Comforting
SOUPS

Colorful
SALADS

**More than 100
Recipes from Spas
and Retreats**

Julie Brinkley

Disclaimer

Everything described in this book is solely for information purposes. The author and publisher make no medical claims or specific recommendations, either direct or implied, for any real or imagined medical, health or body ailment. Always consult your health professional or doctor before you begin any new diet approach or program, or before you add any dietary supplements to your diet. Statements in this book have not been evaluated by the U.S. Food and Drug Administration.

Comforting Soups, Colorful Salads
Published by:
Warm Snow Publishers
P.O. Box 75
Torreon, NM 87061
(505)384-1195

ISBN: 978-0-9710684-6-9

Cover photo by KyleZimmermanPhotography.com

Printed and bound in the United States of America

Acknowledgements

To all those who opened my heart to the pleasures of cooking and to all those that have inspired me. Thank you!

To my Mother for showing me the Southern grace of the cooking art.

To my brother, David, for his unending motivation to inspire and the opportunity he opened for me to share my passion.

To the many people in David's workshops who have tasted my cooking and who encouraged me to write this book.

To all my assistants at David's retreats, who so graciously helped in so many ways.

To my sister, Janice who was my mentor in the kitchen when we were young.

To Jennifer for her persistence in getting me started to write this cookbook.

To Adnan for his purity that seems to touch in so many ways and his encouragement of the spiritual path.

To my daughter Elliiott Marie for her sweet help in the kitchen, so innocently given that continues to inspire me everyday.

To my son Ian Amadeo, who has taken up his own passion of cooking so effortlessly.

To James, my publisher and long time friend, who was so generous with his time, effort and encouragement.

To Katrina, a dear friend and editor, who made my voice come to life.

To my husband Greg, who not only provided the space and time for me to write this book, but also has been a model of the organic way of cooking and living. Greg is the former chief chef and owner of *20 Carrots Natural Foods,* market and restaurant.

My love goes out to you all!

Dedication

To all of you who enjoy the pleasures of cooking

&

to Greg, David, and Elliott Marie

Table of Contents

Foreword

My sister, Julie, is an amazing artist with food, who has inherited from our mother an innate ability to bless her meals with love. This ability gives her food a delicious, nutritious, and irresistible quality. I am fortunate to have Julie handle the nourishment of all the people that come to my workshops. I don't bother asking about the menu, because I know the food will be a highlight. Enjoy this cookbook, because her love is flowing through the menus the same way. Get ready for compliments about your cooking!

David Elliott

Preface

My stomach is growling… Julie is having fun in the kitchen combining foods into a magnificent offering. I can smell it with each breath. Breaths that are getting deeper and more relaxed as the aromas get richer and more tantalizing.

I can hear her scurrying around in the kitchen… dancing really…. and the utensils in the kitchen being used…. Wooden spoons, the knife against the chopping board. The rattling of pots and pans sliding onto the stove top, boiling bubbling liquids, the sound of the oven door opening.

I walk by the kitchen door on my way to my office and take a peek to see counters ablaze in the color of fresh cut garden vegetables, herb and spice canisters… a delightful chaos. A spiral notebook lays open with beautiful handwriting penning recipes and ideas from Julie's hand.

Julie once remarked while smiling … at me… after a meal she had just joyfully prepared, "Food that is made with happiness tastes better, and is far more healing than just plain organic food." I am wondering how much longer it will be before I can sit down to her delicious, healing and happy food and receive her smile from across the table!

Elliott Marie is setting the table and Ian is running out the back door to pick more parsley and cilantro from the garden. These are all signs that the meal is almost complete! I won't have to wait long now. My stomach has grown ravenous in its hunger.

How did Julie come to have such a oneness with her food and its preparation? Was it her growing up on a farm in Kentucky where her Mom and relatives would use any excuse to prepare grand meals? Was it her passion for health that moved her at an early age to choose health foods rather than processed foods? In fact, is it any coincidence that she chose to marry me, at the time I was owner and chef of 20 Carrots Health Food Store and restaurant, where we met? Hum!?

Are we seeing a thread here of many influences that have conspired to show Julie's life long love affair with preparing food? Julie is never happier than when she is sharing her excitement for health and food with her family through her cooking. It is however a happiness that is grounded and focused in her love to bring all the ingredients together for a wonderful meal. The shopping and transporting, the gardening, the harvesting, the cleaning and cutting, the measuring and mixing, the logistics, the singing and the dancing in the kitchen—all of this is the background to her presentation that we simply enjoy.

We are eating and I am nourished with her food—its texture, flavor and color.

As we sit at the dining room table, the well-used recipe book is behind her on the counter in the kitchen. She begins to reach for it to make an entry, but I hold her reaching hand to my lips... as I ravish her smile. Yes... I am responsible for the slight delay in the manuscript becoming the book you are now holding.

But please don't you delay reaching for this book so laden with the unique and earthy rhythm of Julie's creativity. May you too feel Julie's dance in these recipes that they came from!

Gregory Brinkley

Introduction

As great as the recipes are in this book, there is a taste more refined that is more pleasing still to the palette—love!

Love can be tasted in the food we eat by the feeling in the moment, the beauty in the grace of serving and the wholesomeness our bodies feel after a healthy, nourishing meal. These are all recipes for comforting soups and colorful salads.

We can find gratitude and joy in these moments, and finding this, Spirit is transmitted to our food and to our families and friends.

I learned a lot about cooking with love from my Mother, who had all the Southern graces. Cooking became even more conscious after I met Adnan Sarhan, a sufi teacher. He taught me how food can influence the body, the mind and the spirit. With this knowledge, I started to cultivate awareness of recipes and how to serve food which led to being the chef at my brother, David Elliott's retreats. David is author of the book, *The Reluctant Healer*.

Being the chef at his workshops, trainings and retreats, I have learned that the "well being" after a meal is essential so the work can continue and this prepares the body for healing. This opportunity allowed my awareness, my creative flow, and my knowledge of cooking to expand.

My husband Greg and I serve others at our East Mountain Radiant Health and Healing Spa. We encourage healing, relaxation, and well being with healthy food prepared in love.

In this book *Soups and Salads*, we look at soups because of the comfort that they can infuse and salads for their fresh, instilling energy. Who has not felt the warming comfort of a hearty bowl of soup? Who has not found a crisp, colorful salad, refreshing and enlivening?

These recipes always fit the bill and generate good feedback from all. Tasty, nourishing food promotes a healthy body and mind.

You will find that these recipes echo many of today's health-conscious trends without being dogmatic. Again, there is a higher ingredient that we are all beginning to understand as most important in our food… love.

You will be delighted to discover these recipes have simple hints to accommodate or teach wholesome ways of eating. These recipes promote pH balancing, healthy fats, nutrition for well-being, and embrace the vegetarian ideal.

Buy organic whenever possible, support local growers, grow your own! I find my best meals are those that come fresh from a garden. When the food has not only been cooked by loving hands, but grown by loving hands, then the love enlightens the meals.

I hope you will enjoy with your families and friends the many pleasures and benefits that come from making and sharing comforting soups and delicious, colorful salads over many meals.

Julie Brinkley

comforting Soups

Creamy Herbed Potato Soup

Ingredients   *Serves* 4

    1 ½ cup onions, chopped
    1 ½ cup celery, chopped
    1 teaspoon salt
    2 tablespoons butter
    3 cups red potatoes-peeled, cubed
    3 cups water
    1 tablespoon fresh dill, chopped or 1 teaspoon dried (optional)
    1 cup milk
    Fresh ground black pepper to taste

1. In a soup pot, sauté in butter, onions, and celery for 5 minutes.
2. Add salt.
3. Add potatoes, water, dill and marjoram, and bring to a boil.
4. Reduce heat cover and simmer until potatoes are soft.
5. Puree the vegetables mixture with the milk.
6. Salt and pepper to taste.
7. Gently reheat if needed.
8. Serve. Garnish with fresh minced parsley.

Julie's Note:

So soothing, so delicious, this thick, creamy soup is oh-so-easy to make and fits great in just about any menu plan. If that's not enough… the potatoes pack a powerful potassium punch and, just in case you didn't know, they also neutralize body acids which can have a significant effect on arthritis.

Potato Leek Soup

Ingredients *Serves* 6

    8 medium red or white potatoes, peeled and diced
2 teaspoons extra virgin olive oil
3 cups leeks, chopped
1 teaspoon Braggs Liquid Aminos or tamari
2 teaspoons fresh thyme, chopped or 1 teaspoon dried
1 tablespoon fresh tarragon chopped or 1 tablespoon dried
5 cups vegetable broth
Salt and freshly ground black pepper to taste

1. Place peeled potatoes in a bowl of cold water and set aside until needed.
2. Heat the oil in a large soup pot. Add leeks, pepper, and Braggs over medium heat, sauté until leeks are golden brown.
3. Add spices.
4. Drain potatoes and add to mixture and sauté for about 4 minutes until potatoes are beginning to brown.
5. Pour in vegetable broth to cover mixture, add water if necessary, bring to a boil.
6. Reduce the heat and simmer until potatoes are tender.
7. Let soup cool, then puree. Season to taste with salt and freshly ground pepper.
8. Reheat and serve. Garnish with chopped parsley.

Variation: Puree ¾ of soup and add it back to the rest for a chunkier soup.

Julie's Note:

    My Grandmother would make this wonderful, satisfying potato soup, and it really brings back memories. There's a whole lot of comfort here. When I was sick she would always make this for me. It's one of those nurturing soups that folds around your bones and makes everything OK.

    Braggs Liquid Aminos: A liquid vegetable protein made from pure soybeans and purified water. Flavoring similar to tamari. Low sodium content, unfermented, and a good source of amino acids. Certified NON-GMO.

Mother's Taco Soup from Fancy Farm

Ingredients   *Serves 6-8*

2 lbs ground turkey
1 large onion, chopped
Extra virgin olive oil
1- 15 ounce can tomato juice
1-15 ounce can pinto beans or chili beans
1-15 ounce can kidney beans, drained and rinsed
1 10 ounce can Rotel (canned tomatoes and chiles)
2-15 ounce cans diced tomatoes with juice
1- cup fresh or frozen corn
1- 15 ounce can hominy, drained and rinsed
1 can chicken broth
1 pkg. taco seasoning, (a dried dressing mix)
1 pkg. Ranch dressing mix, (a dried dressing mix)

1.   In a large soup pot, sauté onions, cook until onions are golden.
2.   Add turkey and sauté until brown. Add all of the other ingredients.
3.   Simmer on low heat for 2 hours. Season with salt as desired.
4.   Serve with tortilla chips. See page 126 for homemade tortilla chips.
5.   Garnish with shredded cheese and chopped cilantro.

Julie's Note:

When I was real young I started cooking with my mother. I'd help her in the kitchen, and I remember it being that funny combination of chore and passion at the same time. My mother was and still is a great cook and this is one of her favorite recipes. Hearty and good for serving a whole bunch of folk, my mother insists this is one of those ones that's better the second day.

Easily this is a vegetarian soup; just omit the turkey and add an extra can of pinto beans.

Zucchini Soup

6 medium zucchini, sliced
1 cup onion, chopped
¼ cup basmati rice
Chicken or vegetable broth to cover zucchini
1 teaspoon curry powder
1 teaspoon Dijon mustard
1 cup of yogurt
Salt to taste

1. In a large soup pot, combine zucchinis, onions, rice, broth, and water. Add more water, if necessary, to cover ingredients.
2. Simmer until zucchini are tender.
3. Puree in blender, adding enough of the juice from the soup for desired consistency.
4. Add curry powder, mustard, and yogurt and blend into soup.
5. Salt to taste. Serve warm or cool.

Julie's Note:

There's something about New Mexico and squash. They just go together. I came up with this soup to put all that abundance to good use. This soup is so easy to make and great to freeze. Surprisingly the Dijon mustard is that secret ingredient that gives it that special something that makes it so very tasty.

Summer Squash Soup

1 medium leek, chopped finely, using only white part or 1 medium onion
1 pound green summer squash, chopped into 1 inch pieces
2 tablespoons extra virgin olive oil
4 cups vegetable broth
1 tablespoon chopped fresh marjoram or 1 teaspoon dried
4 tablespoons artichoke puree
> *(Make your own by draining a jar of water-packed baby artichokes and grinding them in a blender)*
Salt and freshly ground black pepper to taste

1. In a large soup pot, saute leeks in olive oil until translucent.
2. Add squash, sauté until softens, about 10 minutes.
3. Add broth and marjoram, heat to boiling, reduce heat to a simmer, cover and cook for 30 minutes.
4. Add the artichoke puree and mix well.
5. Let cool (easier to blend). Blend soup into a coarse puree.
6. Season with salt and pepper. Reheat and serve.

Optional: Garnish with Parmesan cheese.

Julie's Note:

If you're looking for something that's low calorie and low carbohydrate, look no more. This soup is also another way to put some of that squash to good use.

Green Pea Soup with Chives

Ingredients   Serves 4

1 tablespoon extra virgin olive oil
1 leek, white part only, chopped
1 white onion, chopped
1 medium zucchini, chopped
1 tablespoon white basmati rice
2 cups fresh or frozen sweet green peas
6-8 whole fresh chives, cut into 1 inch pieces

1. In a soup pot, saute leeks, onion and zucchini in olive oil for about 10 minutes.
2. Add rice and 3 cups of water and bring to a boil. Reduce to a simmer and cover. cook until rice is tender.
3. Add peas, recover and cook until peas are tender.
4. Puree the soup until it is very smooth. Reheat and serve, Garnish with chives.
5. Drizzle with extra virgin olive oil.

Julie's Note:
   Just beautiful to look at, this deep greenness also packs a protein punch. Since fresh peas have a short season, frozen ones are convenient and often make a lot of sense. That said, when fresh are available, be sure to make use of them.
   Try serving this green pea soup in a cup along side any meal, its delicateness is a sure hit.

Ginger Lime Carrot Soup

Ingredients   *Serves 10 one cup servings*

    2 cloves garlic, minced
    ½ cup onion, chopped
    2 teaspoons extra virgin olive oil
    5 cups carrots, chopped
    2 cups chicken broth or vegetable broth
    1 tablespoon fresh ginger, minced
    ¼ cup fresh lime juice
    Yogurt for garnish
    Salt to taste

1. In a soup pot, sauté garlic and onions in olive oil until tender.
2. Stir in carrots.
3. Add broth and enough water to cover the carrots, simmer until carrots are tender, about 20 minutes.
4. Add lime juice, ginger, and salt to taste. Puree soup in blender until smooth.
5. Serve chilled or warm.
6. Top each bowl with a large dollop of yogurt.

Julie's Note:

It took me awhile, but I've learned to love carrot soups, and this is surely a good one to start with. A dear lady who comes to David's retreats, Adrienne, was tasting this soup and said to me, "Wow! This soup is so fresh and alive." The funny thing was I'd actually made it in advance and heated it up from frozen - clearly its life force is a strong one.

The soup is great served with a salad or a sandwich, making a truly satisfying meal.

By the way, if you want to make this ahead of time and freeze it, just hold the ginger and lime-juice until it's unthawed and being heated for serving. If it's on the thick side, go ahead and add a little water.

While we're on the subject of carrots... they're alkaline-forming and clear acidic blood conditions. Also they're one of the richest sources in antioxidant beta-carotene – good for skin tone and treats night blindness.

And let's not forget about ginger; how it aids in digestion.

*Note: If you want to make this soup ahead of time and freeze it, just hold the ginger and lime juice and when you decide to serve the soup, unthaw and during the heating process add fresh ginger and lime juice. May need to add a little water, if too thick.

Sunshine Summer Soup

Ingredients   *Serves 6*

1½ cup onions, chopped
2 tablespoons extra virgin olive oil
1 cup carrots, finely chopped
2 ½ cups sweet potatoes, peeled and diced
6 cups water or 3 cups water, 3 cups vegetable broth
4 cups yellow summer squash, diced
2 cups fresh or frozen corn
½ teaspoon turmeric
4 teaspoons lemon juice
1 tablespoon chopped fresh sage or 1 teaspoon dried
Salt and freshly ground pepper to taste

1. In a large soup pot, sauté the onions in olive oil until translucent.
2. Add the carrots and about 1¾ cups of the sweet potatoes, stir well, and cook for 1-2 min.
3. Add enough water to cover the vegetables, bring to a boil, and lower to a simmer until potatoes are soft.
4. Puree the mixture until smooth and set aside.
5. Next, bring 3 cups of water or broth to a boil.
6. Add the rest of the potatoes and simmer for 5 minutes.
7. Gingerly add in the summer squash, corn, turmeric and lemon juice. Cover, simmer for 10 minutes.
8. Stir in the sage and the reserved puree.
9. Add salt and freshly ground black pepper to taste. Serve. Garnish with grated cheese or sour cream and chopped fresh parsley or fresh snipped chives

Julie's Note:

This soup is an all time favorite. There's something about that fresh sage and lemon juice that sends just about anyone who tastes it to a feelingof comfort. What's more, you can make the puree ahead of time (see step 4) and even freeze it. The day you want to serve it continue with step 5 and add the other ingredients. Wow. Take my word for it, this is a good one.

Springtime Asparagus Soup

Ingredients   *Serves 6*

    1 large onion, chopped
    4 cups vegetable broth
    2 pounds asparagus, snap off tough ends, reserving tips
    4 stalks celery, chopped, including leaves
    Salt and freshly ground black pepper to taste
    1 cup yogurt or plain soy milk or cream

1. In a steamer, steam asparagus tips al dente, take out of steam, place in cold water to stop the asparagus tips from continuing to cook, set aside.
2. In a large soup pot, add onions and broth, bring to a boil and cook for 10 minutes.
3. Add asparagus and celery.
4. Cook until vegetables are tender.
5. Blend the whole mixture until smooth.
6. Return back to soup pot, reheat over medium heat, stirring in yogurt or soy milk or cream.
7. Season to taste.
8. Stir in asparagus tips just before serving.

Julie's Note:

When asparagus hits the farmer's markets, it's a sure sign that Spring has arrived. Light and fresh, this tantalizing, tasty soup holds all that promise of the summer to come. On the medicinal side of things, Chinese herbology recognizes the toning effects of asparagus on the kidneys.

Cool As a Cucumber Yogurt Soup

Ingredients   *Serves 6*

5 cucumbers, peeled and coarsely chopped
2 cups plain yogurt
1 garlic clove, minced
¼ cup fresh chives, coarsely chopped
1 tablespoon fresh dill, chopped
2 tablespoons fresh mint, chopped
1 tablespoon extra virgin olive oil
2 teaspoons fresh lemon juice
Salt to taste

1. Coarsely chop 4 of the cucumbers to make about 5 cups.
2. Combine the cucumbers in a medium bowl with the yogurt, garlic, chives, dill, mint, oil, and lemon juice. Salt to taste.
3. Working in batches, puree in a blender until smooth.
4. Seed and dice the remaining cucumber and add to the soup.
5. Serve at once or refrigerate and serve chilled.
6. Garnish: mint or dill

Julie's Note:

When summer's heat has kicked right in, there's nothing like a bowl of this cool, refreshing soup to take the edge off. Sometimes it's enough in and of itself, the green coolness hitting the spot when nothing else will quite do. Other times I like to serve it with a heavier meal or sandwich. See where the mood takes you.

And as a final note, I've made this one with goat's milk yogurt too and it was just as good.

Ginger Sweet Potato Soup with Cilantro

Ingredients   *Serves* 8

2 teaspoons extra virgin olive oil
1 large onion or 1 leek- white part only
1 carrot, diced
2 lbs sweet potatoes or yams, peeled and cubed
1 inch fresh ginger root, chopped
4 cups chicken broth or vegetable broth
Salt to taste
1 cup plain yogurt
Fresh cilantro, chopped
Lime wedges

1. In a soup pot, sauté leek and carrots in olive oil for 3 minutes.
2. Stir in yams/sweet potatoes and ½ of the ginger
3. Add broth and bring to a boil, cover and lower heat to a simmer until vegetables are soft, about 30 minutes.
4. Blend until smooth. Add salt to taste.
5. Stir in grated ginger.
6. Serve with a dollop of yogurt.
7. Garnish with cilantro. Serve lime wedges on the side.

Julie's Note:

Yum! This is a bowlful of sheer delight. That wonderful blend of tastes and flavors - ginger, cilantro, sweet potato - means that you'll be handing out this recipie to anyone who tries it. Low in carbohydrates and loaded with fiber, antioxidants, and vitamin A, this has got to be one of the top favorites at our day spa.

Provencal Pistou Vegetable Soup

    1 large onion chopped
    2 cups carrots, chopped
    3 medium potatoes, diced
    2 ½ quarts water
    1 teaspoon salt
    Any or all of these vegetables, sliced or chopped:
        1 zucchini
        2 cups broccoli flowerets
        1 cup cauliflower flowerets
        2 cups green beans

    ½ cup broken pieces of spaghetti
    2 slices stale bread shredded

1. In a large soup pot, combine onion, carrot, and potatoes. Add water and salt and heat to boiling. Reduce heat, cover and simmer for 20 minutes.
2. Add zucchini, broccoli, cauliflower, green beans, or any other vegetables of your choice. Add bread and spaghetti and simmer, covered, for 15 minutes more. Season with salt to taste.

Pistou

    8 cloves garlic, minced
    ½ cup chopped parsley, without stems
    1 can (6 oz) tomato paste
    3 tablespoon dried basil, or ½ cup fresh basil
    2 tablespoons extra virgin olive oil
    ¾ cup roasted sunflower seeds or pinon nuts

1. To make pistou, place all pistou ingredients in a blender.
2. Blend garlic, parsley, tomato paste, basil, and olive oil until smooth.

Serve Provencal Vegetable Soup in a bowl with a 1 heaping teaspoon of pistou on top.

Julie's Note:

Italy has it's pesto and France has it's pistou. This is a perfect soup any time of the year. You can also use this pistou recipe on pasta or as a sandwich spread.

Vinny Penza's Minestrone Soup

Ingredients   *Serves 8*

    1 leek or 1 onion, chopped
    1 potato, diced
    1 zucchini, diced
    1 yellow squash, diced
    1 celery stalk, diced
    1 carrot, diced
    2 garlic cloves, chopped
    ½ teaspoon salt
    2 teaspoons fresh, coarsely chopped oregano leaves or dried
    2 teaspoons fresh, coarsely chopped thyme leaves or dried
    1 bay leaf
    4 cups vegetable broth or water
    1-15 oz can diced tomatoes (use Muir Glen fire-roasted tomatoes, if
     available)
    1 cup cooked pasta, elbow macaroni or bowties
    1-15 oz can kidney beans or white beans
    Basil pesto (see recipe next page)

1. In a soup pot saute onions in olive oil until translucent
2. Add and saute potatoes, zucchini, squash, celery, onion, garlic, salt, oregano, thyme, and bay leaf for 10-15 minutes.
3. Add broth, tomatoes, water, and bring to a boil.
4. Cover and reduce heat to a simmer, slowly for 30 minutes or until vegetables are tender.
5. Add pasta and beans, Season with salt and freshly ground black pepper. Remove bay leaf.
6. To serve, pour hot soup in a bowl, top with heaping teaspoon of basil pesto and Parmesan cheese

Basil Pesto (if you make your own)   *Makes about 2 ½ cups*

1 cup packed basil leaves
1 cup packed Italian or curly parsley leaves
½ cup pine nuts or roasted sunflower seeds
6 garlic cloves, sliced thin
¾ cup freshly grated Parmesan cheese
¾ cup extra virgin olive oil

Place all ingredients in a blender or food processor. Pulse the motor to make a homogeneous sauce, which is not as fine as a puree.

Julie's Note:

My friend Vinny from Italy gave me this recipe from his Mom, Gatena. I served it at a Sedona retreat after one of the hikes to Eagle Rock. Eating it was an experience unto itself, each spoonful even more blissful than the last. All of it was gone with not a single drop left.

On the pesto front, you can either make it yourself, or buy it, whichever suits. You can also interchange pesto for pistou – that recipe is on page 28.

Tortellini Artichoke Spinach Soup

Ingredients   *Serves 6*

8 mushrooms, sliced
1 medium yellow onion, chopped
1 can artichoke hearts, drained
6 cups of chicken or vegetable broth
1 16-ounce package tortellini, any variety or flavor
1 pound of fresh spinach, stems removed and leaves coarsely chopped
Optional: grated Parmesan cheese
Salt and freshly ground pepper

1. In a large soup pot, saute mushrooms and onions and olive oil until tender. Season with salt and pepper.
2. Add the artichokes and broth, bring to a boil, add the tortellini, reduce the heat to a simmer.
3. Cook for 5 minutes until the tortellini floats and is cooked through.
4. Fold in the spinach until it has all wilted into the soup.
5. Serve and top with cheese.

Julie's Note:

This recipe is easy, light and fun, especially with the tortellini. Who doesn't just love artichoke hearts! Here is a unique way of capturing their magic.

Tomato, Corn and Basil Soup

1 cup onion, finely chopped
3 tablespoons extra virgin olive oil
6 garlic cloves, minced
2 (28 ounces) canned diced tomatoes, (preferably organic Muir Glen brand)
2 cups water
3 cups fresh or frozen sweet corn
Salt and freshly ground pepper to taste
1 cup fresh basil finely chopped or use dried basil to taste

1. In a soup pot, saute onions in olive oil until the onions just begin to brown.
2. Add garlic and sauté for 1 minute, stirring constantly.
3. Pour in the tomatoes and cook, stirring occasionally.
4. Cover and continue cooking for 5 minutes more.
5. Add the water and corn to the soup and cook until the corn is soft.
6. Season to taste with salt and pepper.
7. Stir in basil and mix well.
8. Serve.
9. May garnish with cheese.

Julie's Note:
Colorful and favorful, this is a favorite with kids. They just love dipping homemade cornbread in it.

Vegetable Soup, the Lemon Cilantro Way

Ingredients   *Serves 8*

1 large onion, chopped
Extra virgin olive oil
3 large carrots, chopped
3 large celery stalks, chopped
5 garlic cloves, minced
8 cups vegetable or chicken broth (can use half water half broth)
2 large potatoes, peeled and diced
½ cup tomato paste (or more to taste)
1 cup fresh or frozen corn
1 cup fresh or frozen peas
1 cup fresh or frozen butter lima beans
1 cup fresh cilantro, finely chopped
6 tablespoons fresh lemon juice or more if desired
Salt and freshly ground black pepper to taste

1. In a large pot over medium heat, saute onions in olive oil until onions are golden.
2. Add garlic and saute for about 3 minutes.
3. Add carrots and celery and sauté for about 5 minutes.
4. Add broth and tomato paste and bring to a boil.
5. Add potatoes.
6. Reduce the heat to low, cover, and simmer until the potato can be easily pierced.
7. Add corn, peas, and lima beans and return to a boil.
8. Reduce heat add lemon juice.
9. Season to taste with salt and freshly ground black pepper. Add cilantro. Serve.

Julie's Note:

When that unmistakable lemon zing is combined with the distinctive cilantro flavor, it's just mouth-wateringly good. What's more, with cilantro helping to cleanse toxic metals from the body, the more the merrier.

Split Pea Soup

Ingredients   *Serves 6*

    2 cups split-pea (rinse 3 times)
    8 cups of water
    Salt to taste

Garnish:
    1 medium onion chopped, sauté in a skillet with olive oil until golden.
    Add 1 cup Hatch green chili, sauté for 2 minutes.
    Add cilantro (1 bunch fresh cilantro, chopped, discarded stems)
    Sauté for 1 minute. Set aside.

1. In a soup pot, bring water to a boil with split peas. Reduce heat to a low simmer and cover. Cook slowly until peas are soft and broken down to a smooth constancy, approximately 2-3 hours.
2. Add salt. Puree if desires.
3. Serve warm in a bowl, garnish with 1 tablespoon of green chili mixture.
4. Freshly ground black pepper is nice too.

Julie's Note:
    Recently I made this at a retreat and realized I had another sure fire hit on my hands. The next week my lovely friend Elsa made it for her daughter, Emma. She loved it too.
    This is another one that you can make ahead of time or in large quantities to defrost whenever you feel like a bowl of warming goodness.

White Bean Soup with Greens

Ingredients   *Serves 6*

1 pound Swiss chard, turnip greens or kale, finely chopped, stems removed
6 cups chicken broth or vegetable broth or water
1 medium onion, chopped
2 cloves garlic, minced
1 tablespoon of fresh ginger, minced
2 cups cooked white beans (drain if from a can)
3 sprigs fresh rosemary, or 1 teaspoon dried (optional)
Salt to taste
1/4 tsp ground white pepper or freshly ground black pepper (optional)

1. In a soup pot, sauté onions in olive oil or water until tender.
2. Add garlic.
3. Add beans.
4. Add broth or water and bring to a boil.
5. Add the greens and the ginger.
6. If using dried rosemary add now. Cover and simmer on low for 30 minutes.
7. Salt and pepper to taste.
8. Serve and garnish with fresh rosemary and drizzle a few drops of extra-virgin olive oil on top, if desired. Garnish with red pepper flakes is nice also.

Variation: Use dried lima beans instead of white beans. Soak lima beans for 8 hours, then cook in water until tender. Add the rest of the ingredients and follow as directed above.

Optional: To have a creamier soup, puree 1/2 of the soup, Stir puree back into the soup, then add greens and continue as directed.

Julie's Note:

One day not so long ago, my friend James was cooking at the Summer Retreat. Wondering what he could add to the white beans, I suggested greens, onions and garlic. And so this soup was born. His creation made with turnip greens caused all 70 folk who ate it to downright rave.

If you've time to make this one using dry beans it's the preferable way to go. First soak the beans overnight, drain off any left over water and rinse thoroughly. Add enough water so that the beans are covered and simmer slowly until they become soft.

Red Lentil Soup

Ingredients   *Serves 8*

    2 cups red lentils (rinsed 3 times)
    Extra virgin olive oil
    1 cup onions, chopped
    4 garlic cloves, minced
    2 teaspoons powdered cumin
    8 cups of water
    Salt to taste

1. In a soup pot, bring water and lentils to a boil, reduce heat once boiling and cover, simmer for about 90 minutes, stirring occasionally. May need to add water if thickens.
2. In a skillet, saute onions in olive oil or in water until golden.
3. Add garlic, sauté for 5 minutes
4. Add to lentils.
5. Continue to cook until lentils are soft and creamy.
6. Season with salt and cumin.
7. Serve warm.
8. Garnish with scallions or a squeeze of fresh lemon.

Julie's Note:

You may wonder at the notion of sautéing onions in water, but once you start you'll see that it's got a whole lot going for it and you won't miss that cooked oil at all. When the soup is ready to serve you can add a high quality, virgin olive oil or my husband Greg's favorite, Udo's Flax Oil, to bring body and nutrition to the meal.

A Purely, Simple Soup

Ingredients Serves 8

2 cups red lentils or split peas (rinsed at least 3 times)
8 cups of water
Salt to taste
Garnish: 6 cloves of finely chopped garlic, mixed with 1 cup of olive oil. Fresh parsley minced.

1. Bring to a boil, water and red lentils in a large soup pot. Reduce heat to a low simmer and cover. This soup can easily boil over, so stir frequently and may want to use a flame diffuser to avoid burning. Add water if soup becomes too thick. You want to cook this until it becomes creamy and smooth.

2. Salt to taste once the soup is creamy. Serve and garnish with drizzle of galic-olive oil, and parsley.

Variation: A nice optional to cooking this soup is to add chopped garlic and chopped ginger half way in the cooking time. When you serve the soup in a bowl drizzle olive oil and garnish with fresh parsley.

Another nice version, once the red lentils are cooked, add ½ cup fresh lemon juice or more to taste. Add 1 tablespoon ground cumin. Garnish with garlic-olive oil and chopped parsley or cilantro.

Julie's Note:

One of the favorites at the Sufi Summer Retreats in New Mexico, this soup comes from the teaching of Adnan whose focus is always on the simple, delicious and healthy. Thanks Adnan!

My friend James is unbeatable when it comes to making this soup just right, so creamy it looks like there has to be butter in it. With there being only beans, water and salt, all the skill is in the slow cook, the occasional stir, and some extra water now and then as needed. That optional final touch of a little ginger or garlic olive oil is a real flavor sensation, and also sparks some good old body warmth.

Curried Cauliflower Soup

1 ½ cup onion, chopped
1 tablespoon fresh chile, minced. Seeds removed for milder taste.
1 tablespoon fresh ginger root, grated
Extra virgin olive oil
1 teaspoon salt
1 teaspoon turmeric
1 teaspoon ground cumin
1 teaspoon ground coriander
½ teaspoon ground cinnamon
2 cups white or red potatoes, diced
4 cups cauliflower florets, cut into bite-size
4 cups of vegetable broth or half water/half broth
¼ cup basmati rice
1 tablespoon fresh lemon juice
1 teaspoon lemon zest
3 tablespoons fresh cilantro, chopped
Salt and freshly ground black pepper to taste
Plain yogurt (optional)

1. In soup pot, saute onions in olive oil or water until the onions are translucent. Add chile and ginger and sprinkle with a dash of salt. Cover and simmer for 5 minutes, stirring occasionally.
2. Add the spices and cook for 2 minutes. Stir constantly to keep from burning. Add the potatoes, cauliflower, water and broth; cover and bring to a boil. When the water boils, add the rice to the pot, cover, and simmer until the vegetables and rice are tender.
3. In a blender, puree about 2 cups of the soup, return to the pot. Stir in lemon juice and lemon zest. Add cilantro.
4. Salt and pepper to taste. Serve topped with a dollop of yogurt, if desired.

Hearty Shiitake Mushroom Soup

Ingredients   *Serves 6*

½ cup uncooked wild rice
1 ½ cups uncooked brown rice
2 tablespoons extra virgin olive oil
1 large yellow onion, finely chopped
3 garlic cloves, chopped
8 ounces of shiitake mushrooms, thinly slices, stems discarded
8 cups chicken or vegetables broth
1 teaspoon chopped fresh rosemary leaves or dried
2 cans (15 oz.) chickpeas, drained
2 cups baby spinach leaves or kale or any greens of choice, finely chopped,
    stems removed
Salt and freshly ground black pepper
1 cup grated Parmesan cheese (optional)

1. In a large saucepan, bring 4 cups of water to a boil. Pour in rice(s) and return to a boil.
2. Reduce heat to a simmer and cover. Cook, without lifting lid, for 45 minutes.
3. Take a large soup pot, heat oil over medium heat. Add onion and cook until tender, about for 5 minutes.
4. Add garlic and mushrooms and cook until tender.
5. Add broth and rosemary and bring to a boil.
6. Add rice and chickpeas and bring to a boil, reduce heat to a simmer and cover, cook for 5 minutes.
7. Stir in spinach or greens of choice and cook until greens are tender. If using spinach, cook until just wilted.
8. Salt and pepper to taste.
9. Serve. Garnish with Parmesan cheese.

Julie's Note:

There's something about shiitakes that means this soup is so much more than just a regular mushroom soup. Their meaty texture and unique, savory flavor transforms this into being closer to a stew. It's also interesting to know that shiitakes are said to be a natural source of the protein interferon, which is thought to boost the immune system.

Roasted Vegetable Soup

    1 pound carrots, peeled and coarsely chopped
    1 pound parsnips, peeled and chopped
    1 small butternut squash, peeled, seeded and chopped
    1 large sweet potato, peeled and chopped
    Extra virgin olive oil
    1 ½ tsp salt
    ½ tsp freshly ground pepper
    3 tablespoons chopped flat-leaf parsley
    8 cups of chicken or vegetable broth or use half water

1. Preheat oven 425 degrees.
2. Place all cut vegetables in a single layer on 2 sheet pans, Do not cut vegetables too small they will shrink. Drizzle the vegetables with 3 tablespoons olive oil, salt and pepper, tossing well. Bake for 30 minutes, until all the vegetables are tender, making sure you turn the vegetables once with a spatula while baking.
3. Sprinkle with parsley after they are done.
4. In batches, coarsely puree one half of roasted vegetables and the broth, using 6 cups of the broth. Cut the rest of vegetables in bite size pieces.
5. Pour the soup into the pot, reheat and season to taste. Thin with the remainder broth to the consistency you like. You may add water if needed. Serve with croutons and a drizzle of good olive
Also, you can coarsely puree all the vegetables with the broth.

Julie's Note:
    Once again, the root vegetables make this soup extra healing.

Greg's 20 Carrots Bean Stew

Ingredients   *Serves 8*

1 large onion, chopped
2 tablespoons extra virgin olive oil
3 garlic cloves, minced
3 celery ribs, chopped
4 carrots, chopped
3 cups of water
1 teaspoon sea salt
1 can (15 ounce) tomatoes and juice or 2 large fresh tomatoes
1 cup green cabbage, chopped
3 cups of cooked garbanzo beans or navy beans
1 teaspoon cumin
½ teaspoon turmeric
1 tablespoon tamari
1 teaspoon raw sugar or sucanat,
> *(Sucanat is organically grown, dehydrated cane juice which some of the minerals in the ane juice are still present).*
1 ½ tablespoon Kudzu or arrowroot powder
Juice of 1 lemon

1. In a large pot, sauté onions in olive oil about 5 minutes.
2. Add garlic, celery, carrots and sauté 5 minutes longer.
3. Add water and sea salt.
4. Cover and bring to a boil over high heat. Reduce heat and simmer until potatoes are tender.
5. Add beans, tomatoes, cabbage, cumin, and turmeric. Cover and simmer.
6. In a small bowl make thickener, combine tamari, lemon, arrowroot/kudzu, and sucanat with 1/3 cup water to form a smooth paste. Stir it into stew and heat for 5 minutes, or until broth thickens.
7. Serve and garnish with chopped scallions, chopped parsley or chopped cilantro.

Julie's Note:

Not so long ago, my husband Greg owned the '20 Carrots' restaurant where he'd always serve a 'soup of the day'. It was there that he taught me about kudzu and arrowroot. Both are natural thickeners and can be substituted for cornstarch in measures of 2 tablespoons of arrowroot or 1 of kudzu for 2 tablespoons of cornstarch. They're also a great substitute for flour.

Imported from Japan, kudzu comes from the root of the kudzu plant and can be dissolved in cool or room temperature liquid. The macrobiotics school of cooking recommends it for its soothing effects on the digestive system.

As its name suggests, arrowroot powder is made from the dried and ground tuberous root of a tropical plant.

As a final note, you can just use a pinch of sugar or even leave it out altogether. There's something about the combination of the thickener with the sweet and sour that really tantalizes the tastebuds.

Great Harvest Stew

Ingredients   *Serves* 6

    1 cup dried lima beans, soaked
    3 cups of water
    2 tablespoons fresh oregano leaves, chopped or 1 tablespoon dried
    1 teaspoon cumin seeds
    ½ teaspoon cinnamon
    1 tablespoon extra virgin olive oil
    1 medium onion, chopped
    1 ½ teaspoons salt
    2 garlic cloves, minced
    3 cups winter squash, peeled and cut into chunks
    1 can (28 ounce) crushed fire-roasted tomatoes
    1 tablespoon chili powder
    1 ½ cups fresh or frozen corn

1. Drain soaking water off beans and rinse. Place in soup pot with water and bring to a boil.
2. Cover and simmer until beans are tender. Approximately 1 hour.
3. May need to add water during the cooking time. Stir occasionally.
4. In a large soup pot, quickly dry toast oregano, cumin seeds, and cinnamon for about 30 seconds. Add oil, onions, salt, garlic, and sauté until onions are soft.
5. Add squash, tomatoes, and chili powder and cook until squash if soft, about 20 minutes
6. May need to add some of the liquid from the lima beans.
7. Once squash starts to soften, add cooked lima beans and corn. Simmer until squash and corn is tender.
8. Adjust seasoning to your taste.
9. Serve hot with grated cheese.

Julie's Note:

A slight chill in the air, a barely perceptible change in the light, the leaves just starting to turn... there are those tell tale signs that the season is changing and with it comes the instinctive desire for warm and comforting foods. With its winter squash, butter beans and fresh corn, this Harvest soup is the epitome of all that.

With corn sold on the roadside in New Mexico during August and September, I buy a whole bunch, shuck and freeze it whole or cut from the cob, and stock up for the year. It makes all the difference.

One other thing... you'll also be glad to know that lima/butter beans have alkalizing properties which are good at neutralizing the kinds of acidic conditions caused from excessive meat and refined food consumption.

Quinoa Vegetable Stew

Ingredients *Serves 6*

½ cup quinoa, rinsed well and drain
1 large yellow onion, chopped
3 tablespoons extra virgin olive oil
2 carrots, diced
2 garlic cloves, minced
1 can (14.5-ounce) whole tomatoes, coarsely chopped and reserve juice
2 cups vegetable broth or water
1 red or yellow bell pepper, seeded and diced
1 zucchini, cubed
1 cup frozen or fresh corn
1 cup frozen or fresh peas
2 teaspoons ground cumin
1 teaspoon ground coriander
1 teaspoon dried oregano
½ teaspoon chili powder
Pinch of cayenne pepper
4 tablespoons fresh lemon juice
Salt and freshly ground black pepper to taste

1. Bring 1 cup water to boil in a saucepan. Add quinoa, reduce heat to very low, cover. Cook until the water completely absorbed and the quinoa is tender.
2. In a soup pot over medium heat, add olive oil and onion and sauté until the onion begins to soften.
3. Add carrot and garlic, cover and cook until the carrots are tender.
4. Add tomatoes with juice. Add broth and / or water. Add peppers, zucchini, corn, and peas.
5. Add the spices. Bring to a boil, cover, reduce heat to a low simmer until the vegetables are cooked to the desired doneness.
6. Stir in quinoa and lemon juice and season with salt and pepper to taste.
7. Serve. Garnish: chopped parsley
   Variation: Add 2 cups cooked pinto beans or chickpeas when you add the vegetables.

Julie's Note:

When I served this stew at a retreat focusing on family, I made a bunch extra. Not only was it was all eaten because it was so very tasty, but I also realized it helped generate a deep feeling of wholesomeness, the kind of togetherness that can be all too rare these days.

It's also good to know that, compared to other grains, quinoa has the highest protein and fat content. It also beats milk when it comes to calcium and is a great source of iron, phosphorous, and E and B vitamins.

Curry Chickpea Stew

Ingredients   *Serves* 8

2 cups chickpeas, cooked
6 cups vegetable broth
2 teaspoons extra virgin olive oil
2 teaspoons cumin seeds
1½ cups leek or onion, chopped
1-2 pinch red chili flakes (optional)
2 teaspoons ginger powder
3 teaspoons curry powder
3 cups sweet potatoes, cubed
1 head of cauliflower, cut into large florets
2 cups peas, frozen (optional)
2 cups coconut milk
4 tablespoons coconut flakes
4 tablespoons cilantro, chopped

1. In a large soup pot, saute leeks or onions with oil until tender.
2. Add cumin seeds cook for 3 minutes.
3. Add the chili flakes, ginger, and curry, stirring constantly for 1 minute.
4. Add sweet potatoes and cauliflower, sautéing until vegetables are well coated with spices.
5. Add the vegetable broth and chickpeas, cover, and bring to a boil. Reduce to a simmer and cook until vegetables are tender.
6. Add peas if desired. Add coconut milk. Simmer until heated through, stirring frequently. Season with salt to taste if needed. Garnish with coconut flakes and chopped cilantro.

Julie's Note:

With the coconut milk, coconut flakes and curry combination, this stew always inspires a slew of praise. When you've got a whole bunch of folk and want a vegetarian option, this is the best. And by the way, the longer it sits, the better it gets, all those flavors just coming alive.

Lemony Lentil Cumin Stew

3 garlic cloves, minced
Extra virgin olive oil
3 cups vegetables broth
2 cups cooked brown lentils
1 cup baby spinach leaves or finely chopped swiss chard
3 tablespoons lemon juice
1 teaspoon lemon zest
¼ teaspoon cayenne pepper (optional)
1 teaspoon cumin
¼ cup fresh mint, chopped

1. In a soup pot, heat oil over medium heat. Add garlic, and cook for 30 seconds.
2. Add broth and lentils, and bring to a boil. Reduce heat, cover and simmer for 10 minutes.
3. Add spinach, lemon juice, lemon zest, cayenne pepper and cumin. Cover and simmer until spinach wilts.
4. Add mint and season to taste with salt and freshly ground black pepper.
5. Serve.

Julie's Note:

To put it simply, lemons, lentils, cumin and spinach are just a really great combination. Try it and you'll see what I mean.

Also, using dried lentils rather than canned is a good way to go, especially because lentils cook far more quickly than other beans. Just remember to soak them first.

Lemons are very therapeutic because they are antiseptic, anti-microbial, and mucus-resolving. Hey, let's eat more lemons.

Root Vegetable Stew

Ingredients   *Serves 6*

2 tablespoons extra virgin olive oil
2 cups onion, chopped
2 garlic cloves, minced
1 cup potatoes or sweet potatoes, peeled and diced
1 cup carrots, chopped
1 cup parsnips, peeled and diced
2 cups turnips and / or rutabaga, peeled and chopped
2 cups beets, peeled and diced
6 cups water
2 teaspoons salt
1 tablespoon minced fresh thyme or 1 teaspoon dried
¼ cup raw-unfiltered apple cider vinegar
4 cups rinsed and chopped greens: beet tops, Swiss chard, kale, spinach, or
     turnip greens
Salt and freshly ground black pepper
1 cup sour cream or plain yogurt (optional)

1. In a large soup pot, saute onions in olive oil until tender.
2. Add garlic, potatoes, carrots, parsnips, turnips, and / or rutabaga, beets, water, salt and herbs.
3. Cover and bring to a boil, reduce to a low simmer until greens are tender.
4. Add salt as needed and add pepper if desired.
5. Serve and optionally garnish with a dollop of yogurt.

Julie's Note:

With all these nutricious and nurturing root vegetables, this is a particularly healing stew that works well at the retreats. The beets, carrots, potatoes, etc., come together in a mouth-watering medley of flavor and texture, and help alkalize the acids that build up in the system. It's a great cleansing for the physical body, beautifully supporting the emotional and spiritual work.

Use raw, unfilited apple cider vinegar not only for its great taste but also for your well-being. The vinegar is the secret to this soup, so don't forget this ingredient.

Hearty Turkey Stew

Ingredients   *Serves 6-8*

2 cups of chopped greens (choose kale, collard greens, or Swiss chard)
1 cup cauliflower florets, cut into bite-size pieces
1 medium red pepper, diced
1 large onion, chopped
3 celery ribs, chopped
1 cup chickpeas, rinsed and drained (optional)
2 garlic cloves, minced
1 ½ pound turkey, chopped in bite size pieces
1 (14 ½ -ounce) can diced tomatoes in juice
4 cups chicken broth or vegetable broth or water
4 tablespoons fresh basil, chopped
4 tablespoons fresh parsley, chopped

1. In a soup pot, saute onions in oil, until tender.
2. Add garlic, cauliflower, red pepper, and celery, sauté for 2 minutes.
3. Add chickpeas (optional), turkey, tomatoes, greens, and broth, cover and bring to a boil. May need to add water to cover vegetables.
4. Reduce heat to a simmer for 20 minutes or until the greens are tender.
5. Salt and pepper to taste.
6. Stir in basil and parsley.
7. Serve.

Julie's Note:

If you're someone who gets tired of all those turkey sandwiches after the holiday feasts, this is a great way to put those leftovers to use. If you've a whole flock of friends and family to feed, you can always serve this with a grain – a nutty brown rice or barley, etc. – and make it stretch a little further.

Gumbo Fish Stew

Ingredients Serves 6

8 ounces red snapper fillet
3 tablespoons extra virgin olive oil
1 cup onions, chopped
3 garlic cloves, minced
2 tablespoons flour
3 cups water or vegetable broth or (½ water, ½ broth)
1 cup carrots, diced
1 cup potatoes, chopped
2 celery ribs, finely chopped
1 cup fresh or frozen okra, chopped or if baby okra, leave whole
½ cup green or red bell pepper, chopped
1 ½ cups canned tomatoes, undrained and chopped
1 teaspoon fresh thyme or ½ teaspoon dried
1 teaspoon fresh oregano or ½ teaspoon dried
1 teaspoon paprika
Pinch of cayenne pepper
3 tablespoons fresh lemon juice
Salt and freshly ground black pepper to taste

1. In a soup pot, combine oil, onions, and garlic, saute until onions are tender.
2. Reduce the heat to low, whisk in flour, cook for 2 minutes stirring constantly. Gradually, stir in water/broth. Cook on medium heat until thickens.
3. Add carrots, potatoes, and celery, cook for 5 minutes.
4. Add okra, bell peppers, tomatoes, thyme, oregano, paprika, and cayenne. Simmer until potatoes are tender.
5. Rinse the red snapper, cut into bite-sized chunks. Add fish, cook for about 10 minutes until fish is tender.
6. Add lemon juice. Season with salt and freshly ground black pepper.
7. Serve and garnish with chopped cilantro.

Julie's Note:

So very good, this is everything Southern wrapped up in a bowl. Also, basmati rice and a wedge of lemon are a great addition. Be sure to have a bottle of Louisiana hot sauce close by.

Autumn Stew

4 cups of onion, chopped
Extra virgin olive oil
2 teaspoons salt
1 teaspoon cinnamon
3 teaspoons cumin seeds
5 tablespoons garlic, minced
3 bell peppers, mix of red, green, yellow
7-ounce can of green chile or fresh Hatch roasted green chile, diced
3 tablespoons chili powder, or to taste
2 cups of water
5 cups of butternut squash, peeled, seeded, chopped
5 tablespoons lime juice or more to taste
zest of 1 lime
2 (15-ounce) cans of pinto beans, drained and rinsed

1. In a large pot, saute onions in olive oil or water, cook over low heat until onions are soft (about 10 minutes). Add salt, cinnamon and cumin.
2. Stir in garlic, chile, and chili powder. Cover and cook for about 5 minutes over medium heat, stirring frequently.
3. Add water, cover and cook for 15 minutes.
4. Stir in squash, lime juice and zest. Cover and cook over low heat until the squash is just tender, but not soft.
5. Stir in the beans, cover and cook for about 5 minutes.
6. Add more lime-juice if needed.
7. Salt and pepper to taste.
8. Serve hot. Garnish is optional: sour cream and toasted pumpkin seeds and cilantro, minced.

Julie's Note:

One of my favorite times of year in New Mexico is when you can find roasters turning green chile in front of most markets. It's also when I take advantage of a finite growing season, stocking up on green chile during August and September and freezing it to use throughout the year.

If you like garnishes, try a dollop of sour cream, a generous sprinkling of roasted pumpkin seeds and a pinch of minced cilantro.

Chili the Vegetarian Way

Ingredients   *Serves 6*

Chili

2 teaspoons extra virgin olive oil
1 onion, chopped
1 red or yellow bell pepper, chopped
2 cans pinto beans or black beans or kidney beans (14 ounce), drained
    and rinsed
1 can diced tomatoes (14 ½ ounces)
1 can (4 ounces) green chile peppers, chopped
2 teaspoons chili powder
2 cloves garlic, minced
1 teaspoon ground cumin
1 teaspoon paprika

Garnish:

½ cup sour cream
1 lime, quartered
Fresh cilantro, chopped
¼ cup green onions, diced

1. In a large pot, saute onions and pepper for about 5 minutes.
2. Add beans, tomatoes (with juice) and garlic, bring to a boil.
3. Add chile peppers, cumin, chili powder, paprika, and simmer for 20 minutes.
4. May need to add a little water if too thick. Salt to taste.

Garnish Salsa:
1 avocado, peeled, pitted, and finely chopped.
1 small tomato, finely chopped
½ red or yellow onion, finely chopped
1 clove garlic, minced
Juice and zest (peel) of 1 lime
A pinch of cayenne pepper
¼ tsp ground black pepper
Salt to taste

1. In a large bowl, combine the avocado, tomato, onion, garlic, cilantro, lime juice, cumin, and pepper. Lightly toss. Let stand for 30 minutes.

Serve chili in a bowl, topped with avocado salsa, sour cream, cilantro, green onions and lime wedges.

Julie's Note:
    For all those chili lovers this is a must. If you're doubtful about the lack of meat, give it a try and you'll see you don't even miss it.

Mexican Chicken Soup

Ingredients   *Serves 6*

Spanish Rice
1 tablespoon extra virgin olive oil
¼ cup onion, chopped
¼ cup celery, diced
¼ cup carrot, diced
1 cup tomatoes, fresh or canned
Cayenne pepper to taste
1 tablespoon paprika
1 ½ cups brown rice
3 cups chicken broth or vegetable broth
½ teaspoon salt

1. To make the rice: Heat the olive oil in large soup pot over low heat, add the onions, celery, carrots, and tomatoes; sauté for 3 minutes, stirring frequently.
2. Add spices, rice, broth, and salt.
3. Cover and bring to a boil, then reduce heat to low simmer for 45 minutes.

Soup
1 cup onion, chopped
1 cup carrots, chopped
1 cup celery, chopped
3 tablespoons extra virgin olive oil
8 cups chicken broth or ½ the amount can be water
1 cup potatoes, cubed
½ teaspoon fresh thyme leaves or dried
3 boneless, skinless chicken breast, chopped to bite-size pieces
3 cups of corn, fresh or frozen
Salt to taste

1. To make the soup: In a soup pot, sauté carrots, onions, celery in olive oil.
2. Cook over low heat until they become tender.
3. Add broth, potatoes, thyme, and salt and bring to a boil.
4. Add chicken.
5. Reduce heat and simmer for 30 minutes. Covered. Add corn. Cook for 15 minutes.

Avocado Salsa

    1 large Hass Avocado, peeled and diced
    3 scallions, chopped
    1 large tomato, diced
    ¼ cup cilantro, chopped
    Juice of 1 lemon
    Juice of 1 lime
    ¼ cup extra virgin olive oil
    Pinch of cayenne pepper
    ¼ teaspoon salt

To serve, place 2-3 tablespoons of rice in each serving bowl, add the soup, garnish with Avocado Salsa.

Julie's Note:

    A whole lot of fun, this soup suits just about everyone. You can be sure you'll be handing out the recipe left, right and center.

Chicken Chili

Ingredients   *Serves* 4-6

3 cups cooked skinless, boneless chicken breast, chopped to bite size.
1 large yellow onion, chopped
1 yellow bell pepper, diced
1 red bell pepper, diced
1 (28 ounces) can of whole tomatoes with juice
1 teaspoon cumin powder
1 teaspoon paprika
1 teaspoon salt and 1 teaspoon freshly ground black pepper
Cayenne pepper to taste.

1. In a soup pot, add olive oil and onions, sauté for 5 minutes.
2. Add bell peppers, continue to sauté for 10 minutes.
3. Add spices and stir in well.
4. Add chicken and tomatoes, simmer on low heat covered for 1 hour.
5. May need to add water if needed.
6. Serve with garnishes of sour cream, chopped cilantro, guacamole or avocado, finely chopped onions, chopped black olives, and chopped chili peppers.

Julie's Note:

One of those dishes that wraps everything up beautifully, there's nothing quite like a warming bowl of chili after an eventful day. This one is simple to make and distinctly tasty, especially if you use those great organic, fire roasted, canned tomatoes by Muir Glen. Also, bare in mind you can always use beans instead of chicken if so desired.

If you're not sure how to roast a chicken, see page 59, steps 1 and 2 for roasting a chicken.

Chicken Noodle Soup

Ingredients   *Serves 6*

4 chicken breast, uncooked, bone in and skin on or 1 whole cooked chicken,
      deboned, skinned and diced
Extra virgin olive oil
2 quarters of chicken broth or ½ water and ½ broth
1 cup carrots, diced
1 cup celery, diced
2 cups wide egg noodles
¼ cup fresh flat leaf parsley, chopped
Salt and freshly ground black pepper to taste.

If you are cooking chicken, this is a simple recipe:

1. Preheat the oven to 350 degrees.
2. Take chicken breast and rub the skin with olive oil. Place the chicken on a baking dish, sprinkle generously with the salt and pepper. Roast for 40 minutes. Let chicken set to cool, then remove the meat from the bones, discard the skin, and dice or shred chicken meat.
3. Bring the chicken broth to a simmer in a large pot and add the carrots and celery. Simmer for about 5 minutes.
4. Add the noodles and simmer for 10 more minutes uncovered until the noodles are cooked.
5. Add the cooked chicken and parsley, heat through.
6. Season to taste. Serve.

Julie's Note:

If you want to serve a light meal but like a bunch of protein, this is the perfect soup. I like to cook the chicken ahead of time or buy an organic, roasted one at the market. If you plan ahead, you can have this meal of nourishing goodness ready in 30 minutes.

Lemon Chicken Ginger Rice Soup

Ingredients   *Serves 6*

1 cup white or brown basmati rice
Extra virgin olive oil
1 large yellow onion, chopped
3 garlic cloves, chopped
1 cup celery, diced
1 cup carrots, diced
1 tablespoon fresh thyme, chopped or ½ tablespoon dried
Salt and freshly ground black pepper.
4 cups chicken broth and or water
2 pounds of chicken tenders, chopped to bite-size pieces
2-inch piece of fresh ginger, peeled and minced
½ cup fresh flat-leaf parsley, chopped
Juice of 2 lemons
Hot sauce, optional
Lemon wedge

1. Cook the rice. 1 cup of rice to 2 cups of water, bring to a boil and add ½ tsp of salt. Cover and turn the heat to low, cook for 45 minutes.
2. In a soup pot, heat olive oil and saute onions, garlic, celery, carrots, and thyme. Stir frequently.
3. Add chicken broth, bring up to a simmer, and simmer for 5 minutes.
4. Add the chicken and ginger, and continue to cook for 15 minutes or until the chicken has cook through. May need to add water.
5. Add parsley, lemon juice and hot sauce to taste. Season with salt and pepper
6. Divide the cooked rice among 4 serving bowls: ladle the soup over the rice, making sure to distribute the chicken and veggies evenly among the bowls.
7. Serve with lemon wedges.

Julie's Note:

Whether you choose to use rice or noodles, chicken soup is always a favorite. If you're serving someone who's not eating wheat, the rice option is a good one. You can also try substituting the chicken for extra firm tofu as a vegetarian alternative. Eating once, eating twice, eating chicken soup with rice.

Thai Chicken or Thai Tofu Soup

Ingredients   *Serves* 4

    4 cups chicken broth or vegetable broth
    1 pound boneless, skinless chicken breast or 1 pound extra firm tofu
            cut into 1 inch cubes
    1 tablespoon lemon juice
    2 tablespoons lime juice
    2 tablespoons ginger, grated
    ½ cup coconut milk
    8 scallions, chopped
    2 teaspoons chili paste
    1 teaspoon fish sauce (found in the Asian area at the market), optional
    3 tablespoons chopped fresh cilantro

1. In a soup pot, start heating the broth while you cut the chicken breast into small cubes or thin strips.
2. Add chicken or tofu to the broth along with the lemon juice, lime juice, and ginger. Bring to boil. Reduce heat, cover pot and simmer for 20 minutes or until chicken is tender. If using tofu, simmer for 10 minutes.
3. Stir in the coconut milk and scallions, and let it cook another 10 minutes.
4. Stir in chili paste and fish sauce. Add salt to taste.
5. Ladle into bowls, top each serving with chopped cilantro, and serve.

Julie's Note:

So very delicious and with that distinct flavor of the Far East, this is a soup that people will ask you to make again and again. And the great thing about that is it's quick and easy, especially if you plan a little in advance and get a pre-cooked, organic chicken from the market on the way home. It's the perfect hassle-free meal for a large group.

Thai Pumpkin-Coconut Soup

Ingredients   *Serves 6*

3 cups pureed, cooked pumpkin, if using canned pumpkin get unsweetened
2 cups vegetable or chicken broth
1 (14-ounce) can of coconut milk
1 tablespoon of miso or tamari
2 teaspoons of curry powder, or to taste
Salt to taste
3 tablespoon chopped fresh cilantro
1 cup toasted coconut flakes
1 cup toasted pumpkin seeds

1. Place pumpkin, coconut milk, and broth in a soup pan. Warm over medium heat until about to boil. Remove from heat.
2. Mix in miso, curry paste, and add salt to taste.
3. Garnish with cilantro, coconut flakes, pumpkin seeds.

Julie's Note:

Again, here's one that's not only tasty, but also real easy to make, especially during the winter holidays. It can be served as an appetizer or a main course, working great either way.

As far as the ingredients go, these days you can find unsweetened, organic pumpkin in the can – how great is that?! Or if you've a little extra time on your hands, you can cook one in the oven as an extra special treat. My husband Greg inspired me by growing his own and then baking them for his recipes, filling our kitchen with smells divine.

Also, if you're unsure where to find curry paste and coconut milk, look in the Asian section at the store. Likewise, Miso can be found in the perishable section. It's a salty paste made from cooked, aged soybeans, and if you find the unpasteurized variety it contains beneficial enzymes that aid in digestion. Stored in the fridge, Miso will keep indefinitely.

If you've ever wondered about curry, it's a blend of spices – usually cumin, coriander, red chilies, mustard, and fenugreek – different mixes varying in strength and potency.

A Healing Soup

Ingredients   *Serves 6-8*

  2-3 garlic cloves, crushed
  1 large onion, chopped
  2-3 quarts water
  Sea salt
  2 carrots, chopped
  5 Brussel sprouts, halved
  1 bunch of dandelion greens, chopped, discard thick stems
  3 celery ribs, chopped
  3 tablespoons fresh ginger, finely diced or grated
  1 bunch parsley, chopped, coarse stems removed

1. In a large soup pot, bring water to a boil. Add onions and simmer until onions are transparent.
2. Add garlic, carrots, Brussel sprouts, dandelion greens, celery and simmer for 15 minutes, covered with lid.
3. Add ginger, parsley, and salt. Cook for 5 minutes. Turn off heat and let sit for 10 minutes, left covered.
4. Serve in bowl and drizzle with extra virgin olive oil or Udo's flax oil.

Healthier variation for preserving the enzymes: Bring the water to a rapid boil, then drop assorted finely chopped vegetables into the water. Cover and turn off heat. Serve after 20 minutes. May need to warm the soup just a little for desired warmth. This would just warm the vegetables, but not cook the vegetables.

Julie's Note:

Soothing stress, easing fatigue and getting you back to feeling right when you might be under the weather, this soup is one I'm very thankful for. While it's good anytime you feel the need, it's especially potent when you're on a cleanse; all those vitamins, antioxidants and alkalizing properties being exactly what you're looking for.

Butternut Squash Soup with Sage

Ingredients   *Serves 6*

2 large butternut squash
Extra virgin olive oil
6 garlic cloves
2 large onions, peeled and quartered
¼ cup water
1 cup apple juice or apple cider, or ½ broth and ½ water
2 cups vegetable or chicken broth
½ teaspoon dried thyme
¼ teaspoon nutmeg
Salt to taste
2 teaspoons butter (optional)
15 fresh sage leaves, finely chopped or 1 tablespoon dried

1. Preheat the oven to 400 F.
2. Brush bottom of a large baking pan with olive oil.
3. Cut squash in halves, scoop out seeds. Lightly brush inside surface of squash with olive oil, place peeled garlic inside squash halves. Place on baking pan.
4. Add onions to pan and brush with oil.
5. Pour water in pan. Cover with foil and baking for 50 minutes or until squash is tender and onions are soft.
6. When squash is cool enough to handle, scoop out the flesh.
7. In a blender, in batches blend squash, onion, garlic and liquid (apple juice, broth or water)
8. Add spices and salt to taste and puree until smooth. Pour soup into pot and heat.
9. Add fresh or dried sage to soup after pureed. If using butter, add now and reheat soup.
10. Serve warm with a dollop of yogurt.

Julie's Note:

Just perfect on a Fall day, this is another soup that gently wraps around your bones and prepares you for the colder months to come. The apple juice works to heighten the flavorful, deep orange-yellow flesh of the squash, and the fresh sage is that special finishing touch that is utterly essential.

Some people say that butternut squash is the most complete food. It's packed with vitamins and phytonutrients (beneficial compounds found in plants) which are said to slow aging, enhance immunity, prevent and slow cancer, enhance communication amongst cells, repair DNA damaged by smoking and other toxins. Super smooth and sumptuous, this soup is also what we all could use a whole lot more of.

Basic Vegetable Broth

Ingredients   *8 Cups*

    2 medium onions, coarsely chopped
    3 large celery ribs, chopped 1 inch slices
    3 large carrots, chopped 1 inch slices
    2 zucchini, coarsely chopped
    4 garlic cloves, each clove peeled
    1 tablespoons extra virgin olive oil (optional)
    6 bay leaves
    Parsley sprigs

1. Preheat oven to 450 F
2. Place all the vegetables on a baking sheet, toss with the oil to coat. Roast for 10 minutes. Stir and roast for 5 minutes more. Do not brown.
3. Transfer the vegetable mixture back to the pot and add 12 cups cold water and the bay leaves. Bring to a boil, reduce the heat to low simmer, cook for 30 minutes, covered.
4. Let stand for 30 minutes.
5. Remove vegetables. Pour through a strainer and reserve broth.
6. Allow to cool. Place in proper containers.
7. Use as needed or freeze in portions, 1 to 2 cups.
8. If you decide not to roast, skip to step 3.

The Easiest Vegetable Broth
Save your cleaned vegetable scraps and simmer in water for 30 minutes and then continue with step 5.

Julie's Note:
  Given that broth is pretty much the key ingredient in soups, it's definitely worth the extra effort to make your own. This is where all the nourishment and flavor happens, and the better the broth, the better the soup. If you make a potfull, it can be stored in a tightly covered container for about three or four days in the fridge. You can also freeze it in handy 1-2 cup servings for up to a month.

Chicken Broth

        18 cups water
        2 pounds of chicken
        2 onions, chopped
        2 carrots, chopped
        1 celery stalk, chopped
        5 garlic cloves, chopped
        1 bay leaf
        Thyme and parsleys sprigs
        6 black peppercorns
        1 lemon

1. In a large soup pot, put all ingredients listed above. Cover.
2. Bring to a boil, stir thoroughly and reduce the heat to low.
3. Gently simmer for about an hour and a half, Remove chicken. Cool until able to handle and remove meat, set aside.
4. Replace chicken bones and simmer for another hour.
5. Remove vegetables and chicken.
6. Ladle broth through a strainer.
7. When broth has cooled, place in proper containers, ready to use or store in freezer for future use.

Julie's Note:

    Again, it's worth the time to make your own, and I guarantee you'll feel really good about doing it too. Also, you'll notice that I haven't added salt to these broths because you'll be doing that when it comes to making the soups – adjusting the seasoning as each recipe calls for it.

colorful
Salads

Pear-Walnut Salad

Ingredients   *Serves* 4

1 head butter lettuce, washed and torn into bite-sized pieces
1 pear, cored and cut into bite-sized pieces
½ cup walnuts, coarsely chopped (roasted is optional)
¼ cup blue cheese or feta (optional)

Balsamic Vinaigrette
2 teaspoons balsamic vinegar
1 clove garlic, minced
1 teaspoon Dijon mustard
1 teaspoon chopped fresh tarragon or 1 teaspoon dried
¼ cup extra-virgin olive oil
Salt to taste

1. Place in a large bowl, lettuce pear, walnuts and cheese.
2. In a small bowl, mix all the balsamic vinaigrette, whisk until combined.
3. Pour over salad and toss.

Julie's Note:
Pears and walnuts combine opposites of flavor and texture just perfectly. Also, a useful trick that helps prevent cut pears from turning brown is to toss them with a little lemon juice.

Fresh Fig and Sunflower Seed Salad

Ingredients   *Serves 6*

    1 head of leafy green or red leafy lettuce, torn into bite-sized pieces
    4 fresh figs, cut into wedges
        (if figs are not in season use dried figs 4-6 sliced or substitute an apple)
    ½ cup sunflower seeds, raw or toasted

Tangy Yogurt Dressing
    1 tablespoon lemon juice
    3 tablespoons yogurt
    Pinch of salt
    Pinch ground cardamom
    4 drops of liquid stevia, or a pinch of powdered stevia or 1 teaspoon honey

1. Place in a large bowl, lettuce figs and sunflower seeds.
2. Whisk the tangy yogurt dressing ingredients together.
3. Pour over salad and toss.

Julie's Note:

Fresh figs are sublime and there's nothing quite like them. That said, dried figs work beautifully too. What's more, not only do they taste good, but they're also one of the most alkalizing foods, easing digestion and acidic build up. You might also find that this salad is just what you need if you're craving a sugary desert, reaping all the nutritional benefits and satisfying your sweet tooth at the same time.

Marge's Endive Salad

5 heads of endive
1 cup walnut halves, toasted dry for about 3 minutes
3 tablespoons raw-unfiltered apple cider vinegar
1 teaspoon Dijon mustard
1 tablespoon mayonnaise, (optional)
1 teaspoon salt
½ teaspoon freshly ground pepper
½ cup extra virgin olive oil
2 cups crumbled feta, blue cheese, or farmers cheese
¼ cup fresh flat-leaf parsley, chopped coarsely

1. Cut the end off each head of endive and peel each leaf off the core.
2. Place leaves in a serving bowl.
3. Whisk together the vinegar, mustard, mayo (if using), salt and pepper in a bowl.
4. Pour over endive.
5. Sprinkle with cheese, walnuts and parsley leaves.
6. Serve.

Julie's Note:

Endive are crisp and succulent and can be found anytime of year making this salad especially good when other lettuce greens are less available and not so fresh.

My mother-in-law, Marge, makes the best salads and this is one of hers. With her years of swimming, tennis playing and good eating, she is the picture of health. There's a plaque in her kitchen that says, 'I KISS BETTER THAN I COOK.' I think she's best at both!

Fennel, Radicchio Salad
with Orange Poppyseed Dressing

1 fennel bulb, thinly sliced
2 romaine lettuce hearts, torn bite-size pieces
1 head of radicchio, shredded
1 granny smith apple, diced
½ cup walnuts, toasted or raw (optional)

Orange Poppyseed Dressing:
1 tablespoon poppy seeds
¼ cup frozen orange juice
¼ teaspoon white pepper
2 tablespoons raw-unfiltered apple cider vinegar
¼ cup extra virgin olive oil
Salt to taste

1. In a serving bowl, place fennel, lettuce, radicchio, and apple.
2. Whisk together, poppy seeds orange juice, pepper, vinegar, and olive oil.
3. Pour over salad and toss. Salt to taste.
4. Add walnuts and serve.
5. May add to the salad, the minced feathery tops of the fennel. This adds a subtle seasoning.

Julie's Note:

Fresh fennel is a stunning vegetable with a distinct licorice taste and a feathery top. I like it so much I'll eat it cut and dipped in lemon juice or vinegarette by itself. It's a member of the parsley family and so it's peak season is from autumn through early spring. It will keep in a plastic bag in the fridge for 4 or 5 days.

Healthwise, fennel is great for harmonizing the stomach.

Romaine, Radicchio Salad
with Lemony Olive Oil

Ingredients   *Serves 6*

    1 head of Romaine lettuce, torn in bite-size pieces
    1 small head radicchio, torn in bite-size pieces
    4 tablespoons red onion, finely chopped
    ½ cup alfalfa sprouts or broccoli sprouts
    4 tablespoons crumbled feta cheese
    1 can of cannellini beans, drain and rinsed (optional)

Lemon Olive Dressing
Juice of 1 lemon
4 tablespoons extra virgin olive oil
2 teaspoons Braggs Liquid Aminos
¼ teaspoon fresh ground pepper

1. Whisk together lemon, olive oil, Braggs, pepper and set aside.
2. In a salad bowl, place greens and radicchio. Add onion and sprouts.
3. Pour dressing over salad. Toss.
4. Add feta and beans.
5. Serve.

Julie's Note:
    Radicchio is that sturdy, burgundy lettuce that we all recognize immediately. It's known for its super sharp taste which is what gives this salad an elegant, extra bite.

Kimchee Salad

Ingredients   *Makes 2 cups*

½ red onion, sliced into crescent moons
1 tablespoon garlic, finely chopped
1 teaspoon extra virgin olive oil
2 cups raw-unfiltered apple cider vinegar
1 tablespoon cayenne pepper, more or less as desired
1 teaspoon paprika
½ head of napa cabbage, chopped 1-inch pieces
2 carrots, peeled and grated
1 tablespoon peeled and grated fresh ginger, more if desired
3 teaspoons lemon juice
2 scallions, chopped
Salt to taste

1. In a large saucepan, sauté onions and garlic until onions begin to brown.
2. Stir in vinegar, removing brown bits from pan.
3. Add cayenne and paprika and boil, until liquid is reduced by half.
4. Add cabbage, carrots, and ginger. Remove from heat. Let set and cool, then add lemon juice, scallions and salt. Serve.

Variation: Omit sauteeing and reduce vinegar to 1 cup. Now you have a live food salad.

Julie's Note:

Super spicy and sour, Kimchee is a traditional Korean condiment that is guaranteed to get your taste buds zinging! Given that this is a live food, it truly begs for lengthy fermentation. The longer it sits, the more those enlivening enzymes just burst with vigor.

Coleslaw

3 cups red or green cabbage (or a mixture), shredded
2 carrots, shredded
¾ cup sunflower seeds, toasted
3 tablespoons mayonnaise or a vegetarian mayonnaise or extra virgin olive oil
¼ cup yogurt or extra virgin olive oil
1 tablespoon lemon juice
1 tablespoon fresh dill or 1 teaspoon dried
Salt and freshly ground black pepper to taste
4 scallions chopped (optional)

In a large bowl, combine all ingredients, except for sunflower seeds. Chill for at least one hour before serving. Just before serving, add sunflower seeds, toss and serve.

Julie's Note:

There are umpteen ways to make coleslaw, and this is the first of a few I want to throw your way. You can make a whole bunch, keep it in the fridge, and dig in whenever the urge takes you, making it a really healthy snack.

There's also the fact that cabbage is considered to be one of the most therapeutic foods in the world. It's been linked with reducing cancer, especially in the colon, and the juice has been proven to help a variety of stomach problems, including ulcers.

Greg's Coleslaw

Ingredients   *Serves 6*

    5 cups shredded cabbage
    ½ cup slivered almonds, toasted
    1½ cups dried cranberries or goji berries
    1 cup celery, diced
    ¼ cup chopped green onions, white and green parts
    ½ cup mayonnaise or vegetarian mayonnaise or extra virgin olive oil
    1 tablespoon sweet pickle relish
    2 tablespoons honey mustard
    Salt and pepper to taste

1. Combine cabbage, almonds, cranberries/goji berries, celery, and green onions in a large bowl.
2. In another small bowl, combine mayo, relish, mustard, salt and pepper, mix.
3. Pour dressing over cabbage mixture and toss.
4. Cover and refrigerate until ready to serve.

Julie's Note:
    Combining cranberries and almonds here you get that fruit and nut thing that is always so good. Also, given the fact that cranberries are rich in antioxidants and almonds (meaning 'all the world' in French) are alkalizing, you've got some seriously healthy stuff in the mix.

Coleslaw with Dulse

    1 head green cabbage, shredded
    3 celery stalks, diced
    3 scallions, chopped
    ½ cup dulse, torn bite size pieces or ¼ cup dulse flakes
    1 cup mayonnaise or vegetarian mayonnaise
    2 tablespoons extra virgin olive oil
    Salt to taste

1. Mix in a large bowl, cabbage, celery, scallions, and dulse.
2. Add mayo, olive oil and salt.
3. Serve at room temperature or chilled.

Julie's Note:

    Being that it's a Kentucky thing, I grew up eating coleslaw and just love it. Cabbage salad was just one of those things we always had – at fish fries, barbeques, you name it, and it was always the salad to eat. I remember putting it on top of my hamburgers too, instead of pickles and lettuce, and now, following in those good old Kentucky footsteps, my family has it on their veggie burgers too.

    The nice thing about using the sea vegetable Dulse is you get that salty, textured goodness, as well as the high iron and mineral content that makes it so good for you. Kept in an airtight container, Dulse will stay fresh indefinitely.

Coleslaw with Blue Cheese

½ head green cabbage, shredded
½ head red cabbage, shredded
4 carrots, grated
3 celery stalks, diced
1½ cups mayonnaise or vegetarian mayonnaise or 1 cup extra virgin olive oil
½ cup Dijon mustard
2 tablespoons whole grain mustard
2 tablespoons raw-unfiltered apple cider vinegar
1½ cups crumbled blue cheese
1 cup chopped fresh parsley leaves, flat leaf preferred

1.   In a large serving bowl, combine cabbages, carrots, and celery.
2.   In a medium bowl, whisk together mayo, mustards, vinegar.
3.   Mix dressing into cabbage mixture.
4.   Add parsley and blue cheese, and toss gently.
5.   Serve at room temperature or chilled.

Julie's Note:

You can always reach for a colorful head of cabbage at the market. If, you like blue cheese be sure to reach for this recipe.

Curried Grain Salad

Ingredients   *Serves 6*

3 cups cooked grain or sprouted grain, (brown rice, quinoa, or grain of choice)
¼ cup golden raisins or goji berries
> *(Soak raisins or berries prior in water 1 to 2 hours until plump and then drain.)*

½ cup almonds, chopped (raw or toasted)
¼ cup fresh flat-leaf parsley, finely chopped
½ cup peas, fresh or frozen, thawed

Honey-Curry Dressing

2 tablespoons lemon juice
2 teaspoon curry powder
2 cloves garlic, minced
¼ teaspoon ground cumin
½ teaspoon ground turmeric
¼ teaspoon coriander
1 tablespoon fresh peeled ginger, chopped
1 tablespoon honey or agave nectar
4 tablespoons extra-virgin olive oil
1 tablespoon toasted sesame oil (optional)

1. In a large bowl, place rice, almonds and parsley. Add raisins or goji berries.
2. Whisk together, dressing ingredients. Pour over rice mixture. Toss and chill for at least 1 hour before serving.

Julie's Note:

This is a salad that can store for six or seven days in your fridge, making it a healthy tide over when you're feeling like a snack. I love the fact that I can put my leftover grains to such good use.

There's also the low down on goji berries (aka Chinese wolfberries); super high in vitamins A and C as well as being the strongest antioxidant food known to humankind. That sounds like a big one, and indeed it is. You can find these berries at www.LoveJoyHealth.com

See agave nectar on page 105.

Quinoa Pilaf Salad

Ingredients

> 1 teaspoon extra virgin olive oil
> 2 garlic cloves, minced
> 1 cup scallions, sliced
> 1 medium zucchini, sliced in thin half moons
> 6 ounces mushrooms, sliced
> 1½ cup quinoa
> 3 cups vegetable broth or water
> 1 cup frozen corn, thawed
> ½ cup Parmesan cheese
> 2 teaspoon Bragg Liquid Aminos

1. In a large saucepan, sauté garlic, zucchini, mushrooms for 3 minutes.
2. Add quinoa, stir 1 minute, add broth, and reduce heat to low.
3. Cover and simmer 15 minutes.
4. Add corn and Parmesan cheese. Simmer 3 minutes or until liquid is absorbed. Serve.

Julie's Note:
Light, fresh and colorful, this one is not only great as a salad or side dish, it's also just plain fun to make. When I put all those great words together, I can't help but think of my cooking assistant at the retreats, Carmen 'the kitchen goddess', who is the epitome of light, fresh and fun.

Lemony Basmati Rice
and Pistachio Salad

Ingredients   *Serves 8*

  2 cups cooked basmati, optional white or brown
  3 tablespoons extra virgin olive oil
  ½ teaspoon ground cinnamon
  ¼ teaspoon ground cardamon
  2 teaspoons lemon zest (peel)
  ¾ cup currants or soaked goji berries (optional)
  ¾ cup roasted or raw pistachios, chopped
  1 cup celery, diced
  Juice of 1 lemon (about 1/3 cup)
  Salt and freshly ground black pepper to taste

1. If serving this dish warm, after rice has cooked, place rice in a serving bowl.
2. Stir in oil, cinnamon, cardamon, and lemon peel. Mix in currants and allow, to cool for 15 minutes,
3. Add the pistachios, celery, lemon juice. Stir well.
4. Salt and pepper to taste. May add more olive oil if desired and serve.
5. If serving chilled, mix all ingredients except for pistachios, refrigerate. When serving, toss and add pistachios.

To toast nuts: Spread them in a single layer on an un-oiled baking sheet and bake in a 350 degree oven for 10 to 15 minutes, stirring once or twice, until lightly brown. *To dry roast:* Place nuts in a dry heated skillett, stirring and tossing frequently until nuts are roasted. Spread on a platter, single layer to cool. Serve at room temperature or chill for 1 hour or longer and serve cold.

Variations: Use orange peel and the juice instead of a lemon. Replace pistachio for toasted almonds. May choose to have the nuts raw instead of toasted. May add 2 tablespoons of freshly, chopped mint.

Julie's Note:

Served warm or cold, this salad is truly wholesome, and has a festive holiday appeal. If you'd like to be extra health conscious, using brown basmati rice ups the stakes in both fibers and minerals.

Chickpea Salad with Mint Dressing

Ingredients   *Serves 6*

2 cups cooked garbanzo beans
1 large carrot, shredded
2 cups cooked brown rice
½ cup parsley, minced

Tahini Mint Dressing
1 tablespoon Braggs Liquid Aminos or tamari
2 tablespoons tahini
2 tablespoons extra virgin olive oil
3 tablespoons lemon juice
¼ cup water or more for desired consistency
1 clove garlic, minced
¼ cup fresh mint leaves or 2 heaping tablespoons of dried peppermint

1. In a bowl, place garbanzo beans, carrot, brown rice, and parsley.
2. Puree dressing ingredients in a blender until smooth. Pour over salad and toss.
3. Best chilled for 1-2 hours.

Julie's Note:
Sometimes it can be a challenge to find vegetarian protein dishes that have a little something extra, and this recipe is a great solution. Using the sesame-based tahini, the milled seeds offer their unique resistance to rancidity, while the mint adds that distinct overtone of special freshness.

Mediterranean Pasta Salad

Ingredients   *Serves 6*

2 cups penne pasta, cooked al dente and cooled
¼ cup sun dried tomatoes, chopped
¼ cup roasted red pepper, chopped
½ cup marinated artichoke hearts, chopped
8 ounces goat cheese, crumbled
20 black olives, pitted and chopped
Fresh basil, finely chopped
¼ cup pine nuts, raw or dry roasted
4 tablespoons balsamic vinegar
5 tablespoons extra-virgin olive oil

1. Mix pasta, tomatoes, cheese, olives and basil.
2. Mix vinegar and olive oil. Pour dressing over pasta salad.
3. Salt and pepper to taste.
4. Garnish with pine nuts.

Julie's Note:

This salad has a whole lot going on. It's got color and a combination of flavors that mean it's not only a dish for the adults, but for the kids too.

A quick note on pine nuts... make sure to keep them in a tightly sealed contained in the fridge or they will go bad pretty fast.

Dry roasted, see page 82, step 5.

Bow Ties with Pesto, Feta and Tomatoes Salad

Ingredients

      1 pound of bow tie pasta, cooked as dente, and drain
      ¾ cup pesto, (recipe on page 31)
      ½ cup pint cherry tomatoes, halved
      1 cup feta cheese, crumbled
      Salt to taste
      Extra virgin olive oil as needed

1. Place pasta in serving bowl.
2. Stir in pesto until the pasta is coated.
3. Toss in cherry tomatoes and feta.
4. Season with salt and freshly ground black pepper.
5. Add olive oil as needed. Serve.

Julie's Note:
    Super simple and super tasty, let's just say that this is one of those salads that people don't easily forget.

Warm Soba Noodle Salad with Kale

Ingredients   *Serves 4-6*

1 package of soba noodles (Eden brand)
1 bunch of kale, stems removed and chopped
Extra virgin olive oil
1 garlic clove, minced
1 tablespoon fresh ginger, grated
2 tablespoons toasted sesame oil
3 tablespoons tamari or Braggs Liquid Aminos
Juice of 1 lemon
½ teaspoon red pepper flakes
2 tablespoons crumbled nori, dulse, or sea vegetables of choice
3 scallions, finely chopped

1. Cook soba noodles according to package directions. Drain and rinse in colander.
2. In a large frying pan on medium heat, sauté kale with olive oil until tender and bright, about 8 minutes. Add garlic and ginger, sauté for 3 minutes.
3. Add soba noodles and toss.
4. Transfer to a serving bowl. Toss gently with sesame oil, Braggs, lemon, and pepper flakes.
5. Serve topped with sea vegetables and scallions.

Julie's Note:

Soba noodles are come in a bunch of varieties and, with their distinct taste and texture, are a nice change from traditional Italian pastas.

One of the most ancient members of the cabbage family, kale is a luxuriant, leafy green that is an exceptional source of chlorophyll, calcium, iron, and vitamin A. It thrives in our garden, and I can pick it fresh even in the coolness of the fall-winter season. Mixed with the noodles, the kale in this salad makes filling meal that warms the body and feeds the soul.

As a last thought, if you like you can add cubed tofu when sautéing the kale.

Asparagus Salad for Two

Ingredients   *Serves* 2

    12 asparagus spears, 1 inch trimmed off bottoms
    5 teaspoons extra virgin olive oil
    1 clove garlic, minced
    1½ teaspoons fresh thyme leaves or ½ teaspoon dried
    ½ teaspoon lemon juice
    2 boiled eggs, sliced into thin rounds
    2 tablespoons scallions, finely chopped
    2 cups arugula or spinach, torn in bite-size pieces
    ¼ cup Parmesan cheese

1. Steam asparagus just tender, but still bright green. Immediately taken from steamer and placed in cold water to stop cooking time.
2. In a serving bowl, place scallions and arugula or spinach.
3. Whisk together, olive oil, garlic, thyme, and lemon juice. Pour over greens and toss.
4. Chop asparagus in half and add to salad.
5. Arrange eggs on top.
6. Salt and pepper to taste.

Julie's Note:

    On those warm summer evenings when there's just a whisper of an appetite, this salad is the perfect light supper.

Watercress Salad

Ingredients   *Serves* 4 as a side salad

   1 bunch watercress, chopped (discarding coarser stems)
   1 English cucumber, halved and thinly sliced
   3 celery stalks, julienned
   1 red onion, thinly sliced
   1 bunch chives, thinly chopped
   ½ cup chopped pecans or walnuts, raw or dry roasted

Mustard Citrus Dressing
   3 tablespoons extra virgin olive oil
   3 tablespoons fresh lemon juice
   2 tablespoons fresh orange juice
   2 teaspoons grated orange zest
   1 teaspoon seeded mustard
   1 tablespoon honey or agave nectar

1. Toss in a large bowl, watercress, cucumber, celery, onion, and chives.
2. Place in a small bowl to be whisk, mustard citrus dressing.
3. Pour over salad and toss.
4. Sprinkle with nuts.
5. Season with freshly ground pepper if desired. Serve.

Julie's Note:
   When I think of watercress, it's the depth of its greenness that always comes to mind. Bursting with chlorophyll, life's force, watercress works on a physical level to correct imbalances and spark renewal just like the promised green of Spring.

Chlorophyll-Rich Herb Salad

Ingredients   *Serves 6*

6 cups mixed salad greens (mixed baby-greens, spinach, and arugula)
1 cup celery with leaves, diced
3 scallions, sliced
1 tablespoon fresh basil, chopped
½ cup fresh parsley, chopped
1 tablespoon fresh dill, chopped
1 tablespoon fresh mint, chopped
1 tablespoon fresh lemon juice or balsamic vinegar
4 tablespoons extra virgin olive oil, add more if desired
1 garlic clove, minced
Salt and freshly ground pepper to taste

1. Combine all greens, celery, scallions and herbs.
2. In a small bowl, whisk oil and lemon juice or vinegar. Add garlic.
3. Sprinkle oil mixture over greens, and toss.
4. Salt and pepper to taste.
5. Serve.

Julie's Note:

All those greens are packed with vitality and when you eat this salad, you are literally eating the warmth and goodness of sunshine. Perfect for after a hike or day at the spa.

Spinach with Portobello Mushroom Salad

Ingredients   *Serves* 4

1 ½ pounds triple washed spinach, coarsely chopped
1 large Portobello mushroom, cut into 2 inch slices
2 tablespoons tamari
½ red onion, sliced in crescent moons
2 hard boiled eggs, sliced in half moons
1 package of tempeh or turkey bacon (optional)
5 tablespoons extra virgin olive oil
3 tablespoons balsamic vinegar
Dash of salt and freshly ground pepper
¼ pound chunk Parmesan cheese

1. Wash spinach, drain and set aside.
2. Lightly spray a medium skillet and sauté Portobello mushroom for 10 minutes or until mushroom softens.
3. Add tamari and cook until tamari is well absorbed, about 1 minute.
4. Season to taste with salt and pepper. Set aside.
5. In a skillet, fry tempeh or turkey bacon until brown and crispy, then crumble. Set aside.
6. In a bowl, whisk together, olive oil, vinegar, salt and pepper for the dressing.
7. In a salad bowl place spinach and top with onions, and mushrooms.
8. Pour dressing over salad and toss.
9. Arrange eggs and turkey or tempeh bacon on top of salad.
10. Season with freshly ground pepper if desired.
11. With a sharp knife or a vegetable peeler, shave the Parmesan into large shards and arrange them on the salad.

Julie's Note:

If you are someone who likes to serve a salad that is a meal in itself, this recipe is exactly that. The velvety mushroom texture and flavor combines with the eggs and spinach to make this wholly satisfying.

Corn, Avocado, and Tomato Salad

Ingredients   *Serves* 4

     2 cups cooked corn, fresh or frozen
     2 Hass avocados, diced
     1 pint cherry tomatoes, halved
     ½ cup purple onion, finely chopped
     3 tablespoons extra virgin olive oil
     Juice of 1 lime
     ¼ cup of cilantro, chopped
     Salt to taste

1. In a large bowl, combine corn, avocados, tomatoes, and onion.
2. Whisk together, lime juice, cilantro, and salt and pour over salad.
3. Gently toss and serve.

Julie's Note:

    This is an all-time favorite and I've served it to countless groups. There's something about the fact that the bright colors make an eye-catching, appealing presentation that is always a good thing when it comes to cooking and serving food. That, and then of course the taste that is just heavenly.

Arugula and Mozzarella Salad

Ingredients   *Serves* 4

2 cups arugula, wash and tear to bite-size pieces
2 tomatoes, chopped
¼ cup purple onion, finely chopped
2 tablespoons pine nuts, dry roasted
¼ cup fresh parsley, finely chopped
1 garlic clove, minced
¼ cup extra virgin olive oil
3 tablespoons fresh lemon juice
¼ cup bread-crumbs
Salt
2 egg-shaped balls of fresh mozzarella

1. To make the dressing, mix together parsley, garlic, olive oil, lemon juice, and ½ teaspoon salt. Set aside.
2. Mix together bread-crumbs.
3. Cut mozzarella into1/2 inch cubes. Place in bread-crumbs and toss to coat well.
4. Spray baking tray with olive oil, place mozzarella cubes on tray, place under broiler for seconds, carefully watching them brown, take out and turn cubes to brown on sides.
5. The trick is to brown and warm them until they become soft and to stop before they become rubbery.
6. In a serving bowl, combine arugula, tomatoes, and onions. Arrange the warm mozzarella cubes on the bed of arugula and tomatoes, Sprinkle with pine nuts. Drizzle the dressing over top and serve.

Julie's Note:

The warm mozzarella toasted in breadcrumbs gives this salad a fancy feel that can't help but impress, especially once it has been tasted. For a slightly stronger flavor, you can also try using a firm goat's cheese.

Because they can add so much to a dish, bread crumbs are a handy ingredient to have around. They're also another of those things that, whenever possible, should be home-made.

My Family's Favorite Salad in the Hamptons

Ingredients   *Serves 6*

> 4 medium tomatoes or 6 small tomatoes
> Basil leaves
> 1 pound of fresh mozzarella
> Extra virgin olive oil
> Sea salt
> Freshly ground black pepper

1. Slice tomatoes and mozzarella in thin circles.
2. Arrange on platter, alternating tomato, mozzarella, and basil.
3. Drizzle with olive oil.
4. Sprinkle with salt and pepper.
5. Serve at room temperature.

Julie's Note:

When the summertime rolls around, our family loves to visit my husband's sister, Christie, in the Hamptons. The long, sultry, beachside days wouldn't be quite the same without this salad – always made with fresh basil and tomatoes from Christie's garden.

Oftentimes the basil we get in the summer comes in thriving stems covered in leaves. The best way to clean it is to pick the leaves, wash and pat them dry or spin in a salad spinner, and then store in a closed plastic bag with a dry paper towel in the fridge. That way you can make use of all their bounty without them turning brown right away.

Ricotta Egg Salad

Ingredients   *Yield: 2 cups*

    ½ cup fresh parsley, finely minced
    2 tablespoons grated lemon zest
    1 tablespoon garlic, minced
    ½ teaspoon salt
    ½ cup ricotta cheese
    8 hard-boiled eggs, allow to cool then chop

1. Combine the parsley, lemon zest, and garlic in a bowl.
2. Add eggs, salt, and ricotta cheese.
3. Mix well. Cover tightly and refrigerate for 1 hour.

Julie's Note:

To serve, spread on crackers, bagel chips or cucumber slices or just onto a piece or crusty bread. You can also add some freshly ground black pepper and a touch of minced olives.

Egg Salad with Watercress and Smoked Salmon

Ingredients   *Yields 2 cups*

6 hard-boiled eggs
1 tablespoon shallot or purple onion, finely chopped
2 teaspoons tarragon leaves, finely chopped or 1 teaspoon dried
½ teaspoon celery seeds
¼ cup mayonnaise or more if desired
Salt and freshly ground black pepper to taste
Watercress sprigs, tough stems discarded
Smoked salmon sliced, optional

1. Mash eggs coarsely with a fork.
2. Mix in onion, tarragon, celery seed, mayo, and salt and pepper to taste.
3. Make sandwiches with any type of bread, roll or cracker you wish, top with egg salad, watercress and salmon.

Julie's Note:
   If you want to lower the fat, discard as many egg yolks as you want.

Tofu Eggless Salad

Ingredients *Serves 6*

    2 cakes of tofu
    ½ cup dill pickle relish
    2 tablespoons mustard
    ½ teaspoon salt
    ½ cup mayonnaise or vegetarian mayonnaise
    Dash of turmeric
    1 green onion, finely chopped

1. Crumble or mash tofu into a bowl.
2. Add all the other ingredients
3. Mix together.
4. Chill before serving.

Optional: Simmer tofu in water for 5 minutes to make it more digestible and encourage the flavors of the remaining ingredients to blend.

Tofu Salad

Ingredients   *Serves* 4

    2 teaspoons sweet chili sauce
    1 teaspoon fresh ginger, minced
    2 teaspoons Braggs Liquid Aminos
    2 tablespoons sesame oil
    9 ounces firm tofu
    1 cup snow peas, julienned
    2 carrots, julienned
    1 ½ cups red cabbage, finely shredded
    2 tablespoons peanuts, chopped, (unsalted works best)

1. Put chili sauce, ginger, Braggs, and sesame oil in a small bowl and whisk.
2. Cut the tofu into 1-inch cubes and place in a bowl.
3. Pour the marinade over, stir well, and cover. Refrigerate for 1 hour.
4. Blanch the snow peas for 1 minute. Drain and plunge into ice water, and drain again.
5. Add the snow peas to the tofu with the carrots and cabbage and toss to combine. Sprinkle with peanuts. Serve.

Julie's Note:

If you're already a vegetarian, or becoming one, this is a great 'transitional' meal. It's also perfect to serve to a large group when there are non-meat eaters in the mix as it's a recipe that everyone always seems to enjoy.

Coming into our culture more and more, tofu is processed soybean curd that's full of B-vitamins, calcium, phosphorous, iron, sodium, and potassium. It's inexpensive and, because it's relatively high in protein, is often used instead of meat. When you can, it's best to buy it organic.

Moroccan Carrot Salad

Ingredients   *Serves 6*

  6 carrots, grated
  1 bunch cilantro, finely chopped
  4 tablespoons pistachio nuts or nuts of choice, chopped
  2 tablespoons orange juice
  1 ½ cups plain yogurt or goat yogurt
  2 cardamom pods
  1 teaspoon black mustard seeds
  ½ teaspoon ground cumin
  ½ teaspoon ground ginger
  1 teaspoon paprika
  ½ teaspoon ground coriander
  ¼ cup currants or goji berries, soaked until plump
  6 tablespoons extra virgin olive oil
  Juice of 1 lemon

1. Crush the cardamom pods to extract the seeds, discard the pods.
2. Heat a frying pan over low heat and dry-fry the mustard seeds for a few seconds or until they start to pop.
3. Add all the dry spices and cook for 10 seconds or until fragrant.
4. Remove from heat and stir in the currants, oil, lemon juice and orange juice.
5. Place in a large bowl, carrots.
6. Mix in the spice mixture, cover and set aside for 30 minutes.
7. Then mix in the yogurt. Sprinkle with the pistachios. Serve.

Julie's Note:

  With a little of this and a little of that, you can take a regular carrot salad and make it something pretty exceptional. I'd even go as far to say that this one is truly exotic! See page 80 about goji berries.

Middle Eastern Beet Salad

Ingredients   *Serves* 4

    4 large beets, peeled and cut in ½ inch half-moons
    1 tablespoon fresh scallions, chopped
    3 tablespoons fresh cilantro, chopped
    2 garlic cloves, minced
    ½ fresh chile, seeded and minced, optional
    1 teaspoon ground cumin
    3 tablespoons lemon juice
    4 tablespoons extra virgin olive oil, more if needed
    Salt to taste

1. In a large pot, place beets in pot and cover with water and bring to a boil. Cover and reduce heat to a simmer. Cook until tender, easy pierced with a knife.
2. When, beets are cooked, drain and transfer to a serving bowl.
3. Add scallions, cilantro, garlic, chile, cumin, lemon juice, oil, and salt. Toss well.
4. Best to chill for at least 1 hour before serving.

Julie's Note:

There have been numerous times when people have told me they don't like beets. That's before they've tasted this salad. If you're someone who has a questionable relationship with beets, definitely make the effort to give this salad a try. The exceptional blood-purifying effects (betrayed by the vegetable's rich redness) alone make it worth your while.

Beets, Feta and Watercress Salad with Shallot and Thyme Dressing

> 8 medium beets
> ¼ cup feta cheese
> 1 bunch watercress, discard thick stems

> **Olive Thyme Dressing:**
> ½ cup extra virgin olive oil
> 1 large shallot, finely chopped
> Juice of 1 lemon
> Leaves from 10 sprigs of thyme or 1 tablespoon dried
> Salt and freshly ground black pepper to taste

1. Cook beets in water to cover until tender, about 40-45 minutes. Drain the beets and set aside to cool. When the beets are cool enough to handle, use a knife and peel off the beet skins. Cut the beets into cubes. Place in a serving bowl.
2. To make the dressing, whisk together olive oil, shallot, lemon juice, thyme, salt and pepper. Set aside.
3. Wash the watercress, remove leaves from the thick stems. Toss watercress with the beets, add dressing, and toss gently. Crumble the cheese on top.
4. Serve.

Julie's Note:
   The array of red and green in this salad, coupled with the potent health qualities each vegetable brings, makes this beautiful to look at, nutricious to eat, and delicious to taste.

Lively Carrot-Beet Salad

Ingredients   *Serves* 8

      10 large raw carrots, grated
      4 raw beets, grated
      ½ cup raisins or goji berries, soaked until plump
      ¼ cup extra virgin olive oil
      Juice or 1 lemon
      10 mint leaves, chopped
      Salt to taste

1. 1 hour prior to making the salad, soak raisins or berries in 1 cup of water.
2. Whisk in a bowl the dressing: oil, lemon juice, and salt.
3. In a large bowl combine carrots, beets, and toss with the dressing.
4. Drain the raisins and add to the salad. Add mint.
5. Refrigerate or serve immediately.
6. Garnish with sunflower sprouts.

Julie's Note:

    When you eat raw food, you eat the living enzymes, transferring their life force to yours. Overflowing with antioxidants, vitamins and minerals, this salad both nurtures the body as well as acting as a great intestinal cleanser.

Succulent Rainbow Salad

Ingredients   *Serves 8 (4 if serving for as a main course)*

½ head romaine lettuce
1 bunch spinach
½ bunch arugula
1 cup radicchio, shredded
1 granny smith apple, cut into bite-sized pieces
1 avocado, cut in bite-sized pieces
3 scallions, finely sliced
1 cup bean sprouts or alfalfa sprouts
2 raw beets, grated
½ large jicama, grated
2 carrots, grated
3 Roma tomatoes, chopped
¼ cup raw or toasted nuts or seeds of your choice

Wash and tear greens to bite-sized pieces. Place in serviing bowl. Add all other ingredients, arranging vegetables like a rainbow.

Lemony Garlic Flax Dressing:

1 cup extra virgin olive oil
¼ cup flax oil
1 garlic clove, minced
Juice of 1 lemon
¼ cup Braggs Liquid Aminos or 1 teaspoon salt

In a small bowl, whisk together all dressing ingredients. Set aside. Add dressing just before serving or pass it at the table.

Julie's Note:

For me this salad has always been like a beautiful work of art. The various colors remind me of the rainbows we see here in New Mexico, and from that spectrum of hues also comes the notion that different colors support and balance the energy of the body. The grating of the vegetables unleashes their natural sweetness.

There's many ingredients that could be played with, and I hope once you try it, you'll improvise your own versions.

Zesty Green Bean Salad

Ingredients   *Serves 6*

1 pound green beans, trimmed and cut into bite-size pieces
¼ cup extra virgin olive oil or more if desired
3 tablespoons fresh dill, chopped or 2 tablespoons dried
2 teaspoons raw-unfiltered apple cider vinegar
Grated zest of 1 lemon and the juice of 1 lemon
Salt and freshly ground black pepper to taste.

1.   Steam the green beans until just tender and bright green.
2.   Immediately after removing from the heat, shock them in cold water and drain
      thoroughly in a colander.
3.   Whisk together the oil, lemon zest and juice, dill, vinegar in a bowl.
4.   Toss the beans with the dressing.
5.   Salt and pepper to taste.
6.   Chill and toss again before serving.

Make extra for the next day to put in a fresh green salad.

Julie's Note:

I grew up picking bushels of green beans every summer from my
Grandparents garden. It was one of those things that just became akin to
that fresh, earth smell and a certain kind of feeling that was summer itself.
   One of the things I love about green beans is that there's a whole
bunch of ways to cook 'em. When this cool, zesty salad is accompanied by a
light soup and hunk of good bread, it's just perfect on a summer's day.

Honey Mustard Green Bean Vinaigrette Salad

Ingredients   *Serves 6*

> 5 cups green beans, stem and snap in halves,
> 8 cups of water
> 1 teaspoon salt
> ¼ cup fresh lemon juice
> 2 tablespoons extra virgin olive oil
> 1 tablespoon Dijon mustard
> 1 tablespoon honey or agave nectar
> 2 tablespoons purple onion, finely chopped
> ¼ cup silvered almonds
> Salt and freshly ground black pepper to taste

1. In a saucepan, combine water and salt and bring to a rolling boil.
2. Drop green beans in boiling water for about 5 minutes or just until soft.
3. Drain the green beans and place them in a serving bowl.
4. In a small bowl, whisk together, lemon juice, mustard, oil, mustard, and honey and onion.
5. Pour dressing over the green beans and toss well.
6. Salt and pepper to taste.
7. Add almonds. Serve.

Julie's Note:

Again, this is a salad that harness the freshness and taste of summer.

If you're unsure about agave nectar, it's from the agave tequilana plant and can be used as a natural low-glycemic sweetener for just about anything you want to eat or drink.

Fiesta Cucumber Salad

Ingredients   *Serves 6*

     3 medium cucumbers
     ½ red onion, finely sliced

Fiesta Dressing:
     ½ cup raw-unfiltered apple cider vinegar
     1 tablespoon tamari or Braggs Liquid Aminos
     1 tablespoon honey, agave nectar, succant or raw sugar
     ½ fresh green chile, seeded and minced
     ¼ teaspoon freshly ground black pepper
     2 teaspoons fresh ginger, minced
     Salt to taste.
     Optional: coarsely chopped roasted peanuts

1. Peel the cucumbers, halve them lengthwise, and scoop out the seeds with a spoon.
2. Slice the cucumbers crosswise into ½ inch-thick crescents.
3. Add the cucumbers and the onions and set aside.
4. Stir together the vinegar, tamari, sugar, chile, black pepper, and ginger in a bowl.
5. Pour the dressing over the cucumbers and onions. Toss and add salt if desired. Refrigerate.
6. Serve chilled, garnish with peanuts

Julie's Note:
     Cucumber is one of the most alkalizing foods that you can eat. It is considered to have a cooling and purifying effect on the digestive system and is very beneficial to the hair and skin. This crisp and spicy salad is a treat, almost no fat, great addition to any meal. May not need to salt if using salted peanuts.

Summery Cucumber Tomato Salad

Ingredients   *Serves* 4

1 cucumber, peeled, seeded and sliced
2 vine ripe tomatoes, diced
1 bunch of flat-leaf parsley, chopped
½ purple onion, chopped
2 tablespoons raw-unfiltered apple cider vinegar, or a couple of splashes, more if desired
3 tablespoons extra virgin olive oil
Salt and freshly ground black pepper to taste

1. Combine cucumber, tomato, parsley, and onion in a salad bowl.
2. Dress with vinegar, olive oil, salt and pepper to your taste.
3. Serve or refrigerate for later.

Julie's Note:

I add tomatoes and parsley to give it a little more color and deliciousness.

Cucumber Salad from Kentucky

Ingredients   *Serves* 4

1 large cucumber, peeled and sliced
½ white raw onion, sliced into crescent moons
Splash of white vinegar
Salt and pepper to taste
Pinch of succanat or raw organic sugar (optional)

1.   Combine all ingredients and toss.
2.   Cover and chill.
3.   Serve at lunch or dinner.
4.   The longer this salad marinates the better it taste.

Julie's Note:

This is such a fresh, juicy salad. Growing up in the summers in Kentucky, every day we would have a fresh cucumber salad along with our meals for lunch or dinner.

Red Potato Salad with Asparagus and Artichoke Hearts

Ingredients *Serves* 8

3 pounds of red potatoes, quartered (15 small or 9 large)
1 pound of fresh asparagus, 1 inch trimmed off the base
4 tablespoons raw-unfiltered apple cider vinegar
1 teaspoon Dijon mustard
1 teaspoon honey or agave nectar
6 tablespoons extra virgin olive oil
1 can (14-ounce) whole artichoke hearts, drained and quartered
3 ounces blue cheese or feta, crumbled (optional)
2 tablespoons chopped fresh dill or parsley
3 scallions, chopped (optional)
Salt and freshly ground black pepper to taste

1. In a large pot, place potatoes and enough water to cover and bring to a boil.
2. Reduce heat to low, cover and simmer until they can be pierced with a fork.
3. Drain and let cool.
4. Steam the asparagus until tender, 8 minutes. Immediately remove from the steamer, place in cold water for a few minutes.
5. Transfer to a cutting board and slice into 1-inch lengths and add to the potatoes.
6. Whisk together the vinegar, mustard, honey, and oil. Whisk until creamy.
7. Add the artichokes and dressing to the potatoes and toss.
8. Add cheese, dill, and scallions. Salt and pepper to taste. Toss lightly
9. Refrigerate until serving time

Julie's Note:

Hearty and somewhat substantial, this is a salad that I love to serve as a compliment to a simple main dish like grilled fish or chicken.

This is also a good opportunity to remind about the wholesome goodness of potatoes. They are a key ingredient to helping to neutralize body acids which, when they are in excess, are said to cause disease and infection. If you're curious to know more about acid-alkaline balance, *The Ph Miracle Book* is a great resource.

Baked Potato Filled with Salad

4 large baking potatoes
1 cup frozen corn or fresh corn
2 celery stalks, sliced
2 cups baby spinach leaves, arugula, or fresh chopped greens of choice
Optional: smoked salmon, break into small pieces and or grated cheese
Salt and freshly ground black pepper to taste

Tomato, Oil and Vinegar Dressing:

4 tablespoons tomato juice
3 tablespoons vinegar
4 tablespoons extra virgin olive oil

1. Preheat the oven 400 F. Thoroughly scrub the skins of the potatoes and prick them several times. Rub salt on the potato skin all over while the potato is wet.
2. Place on baking sheet, uncovered for 1 hour or until tender when pierced with a sharp knife.
3. To make the dressing, whisk all the dressing ingredients in a small bowl. Season with salt and pepper and set aside.
4. Place the potatoes on a chopping board and cut the potatoes deep down the middle, be careful not to cut all the way through.
5. Put the corn, celery, and fresh greens in a large bowl, toss with the dressing. Salt and pepper to taste.
6. Place the potatoes on a serving plate. Spoon the salad mixture into each potato.

Julie's Note:

Optional: Top with salmon or grated cheese to create a whole meal.

Mustard Potato Salad

Ingredients   *Serves 6*

3 pounds small red or Yukon potatoes
Salt
1 ¼ cups mayonnaise or vegetarian mayonnaise or 1 cup extra virgin olive oil
4 tablespoons Dijon or French style mustard
½ cup fresh dill, chopped
½ cup celery, diced
½ cup onion, diced
2 tablespoons dill pickle relish
Freshly ground black pepper to taste

1. Place potatoes and 2 tablespoons salt in a large pot of water. Bring to a boil, then lower heat and simmer until potatoes are barely tender when pierced with a knife. Drain potatoes in a colander. Place colander with the potatoes over an empty pot, cover and allow to drain.
2. In a small bowl, whisk together mayo, mustard, dill, 1 teaspoon salt, and 1 teaspoon pepper. Set aside.
3. Take potatoes and cut them into quarters or halves depending on their size.
4. Place in a large bowl.
5. Pour dressing over the cut potatoes.
6. Add celery, onions, and relish.
7. Add salt and pepper to taste.
8. Toss well, cover and refrigerate for a few hours to allow the flavors to blend.
9. Serve cold or at room temperature.

Warm Dijon Potato Salad
with Green Beans

3 pounds Yukon potatoes
1 pound green beans, trimmed
½ cup mayonnaise or vegetarian mayonnaise or extra virgin olive oil
2 tablespoons whole grain Dijon mustard
1 shallot, minced
3 tablespoons raw-unfiltered apple cider vinegar
½ cup packed finely chopped flat-leaf parsley

1. Place potatoes in a large pot and cover with water and salt, bring to a boil and cook until the potatoes are fork tender. Drain and rinse under cold water.
2. Bring another pot of salted water to a boil, add green beans carefully watching for beans to turn bright green. Strain beans and run them under cold water to stop the beans from cooking.
3. In a mixing bowl combine the remaining ingredients and whisk until smooth.
4. Dice potatoes into 1 inch chunks. Cut beans in half.
5. Toss the potatoes in the dressing.
6. Add green beans and parsley and toss.
7. Serve.

Steve's Favorite Potato Salad

Ingredients   *Serves 6*

2 pounds small, red skinned potatoes or Yukon gold
¼ cup extra virgin olive oil, more if needed
¼ cup lemon juice, more if desired
2 cloves garlic, minced
¼ cup parsley, chopped
¼ cup scallions, chopped
¼ cup celery, diced
Salt and freshly ground black pepper to taste

1. In a large saucepan, place washed potatoes in pan with enough water to cover.
2. Bring to boil over high heat, reduce the heat to medium-low, cover, and simmer until potatoes are tender when pierced with a knife, about 15 minutes. Do not over cook.
3. Drain potatoes. As soon as potatoes are cool enough to handle, quarter them.
4. In a bowl, whisk together the olive oil, lemon juice, garlic, salt and pepper.
5. Pour dressing over potatoes and toss gently. Add more olive oil or lemon to your desired taste.
6. Add parsley, scallions, and celery to salad, tossing gently.
7. Serve the salad warm or at room temperature.
8. Salad is also delicious cold.

Optional: Add chopped spinach or romaine lettuce.

Julie's Note:

The flavors of this salad are tangy and robust without the excessive fat and calories of mayonnaise. My dear friend, Steve Crespo, really likes this salad, so I named this salad after him.

Yam-Potato Salad

Ingredients   *Serves* 4

      2 medium yams or sweet potatos
      2 medium Yukon gold potatoes
      ½ teaspoon cumin seeds
      ¼ teaspoon peppercorns
      A pinch of cayenne pepper
      Salt to taste
      1½ cup plain yogurt, (cow, goat or soy)
      2 tablespoons pistachios, coarsely chopped
      ¼ teaspoon paprika, sweet or hot
      2 tablespoons minced mint leaves, optional

1. In a saucepan, place yam and potato and cover with salted water and bring to a boil.
2. Reduce heat to a simmer and cook until tender.
3. Drain potatoes and cool slightly, then peel and dice. Set aside.
4. In a dry skillet over medium heat, toast cumin and peppercorns, shake and stir frequently until aromatic, about 5 minutes. Transfer spices to a grinder and grind until a coarse powder.
5. In a bowl, combine cumin- pepper mixture, and cayenne.
6. Blend in yogurt and fold in potatoes. May add more yogurt for desired consistency.
7. Salt to taste.
8. Sprinkle with pistachios, paprika, and mint.
9. Serve at room temperature or chilled.

Julie's Note:

    Something tells me that sweet potatoes, like potatoes, don't usually get their full due. Packed with vitamin A and known in Chinese medicine to promote Qi (pronounced 'chee' and sometimes spelled Chi), the vital essence or life force found in all things, they're one of those vegetables that we should just be eating up.

Alexander's Greek Salad

Ingredients   *Serves* 4

    4 Roma tomatoes, cut into wedges
    1 English cucumber, peeled, halved, seeded, and diced into small cubes
    2 bell peppers, cut into matchsticks
    ¼ cup red onions, sliced half rings
    16 kalamati olives, halved
    9 oz. firm feta cheese, cubed
    2 hearts of romaine lettuce, chopped
    ¼ cup flat-leaf parsley, chopped
    12 mint leaves, chopped
    ½ teaspoon fresh oregano, chopped or ½ teaspoon dried
    ½ cup extra virgin olive oil
    Juice of 1 lemon
    2 cloves garlic, crushed and minced

1. Place in a large serving bowl, tomatoes, cucumbers, bell peppers, onion, and olives.
2. In a bowl, combine olive oil, lemon juice, garlic and oregano.
3. Pour dressing over the salad, and toss well.
4. Mix in mint and parsley and feta and toss gently.
5. Salt and freshly ground black pepper to taste.
6. Serve.

Julie's Note:

A good friend in Philadelphia had a Middle Eastern restaurant that was once voted the best in town. This recipe comes from him. Given that there's a variety of fetas to choose from, you should know that Alex liked Bulgarian feta the best.

Fava Bean Salad

*Ingredients**Serves* 4

    2 cans foul mudammas
        *(fava beans found in the international section at the grocery or at a
        Middle Eastern grocery)*
    ¼ cup scallions, chopped
    ¼ cup parsley, chopped
    2 tablespoons fresh mint, chopped
    2 cloves garlic, minced
    2 Roma tomatoes, diced
    ¼ cup extra virgin olive oil
    ¼ cup lemon juice
    3 tablespoons pomegranate molasses
        *(found in the international section at the grocery or at a Middle
        Eastern grocery)*
    Salt to taste

1. In a saucepan on medium-high heat warm up the 2 cans of foul.
2. Once hot, drain off liquid from beans and place beans in a large bowl.
3. Add scallions, parsley, mint, garlic, and tomatoes. Toss.
4. Add olive oil, lemon juice, and pomegranate molasses. Add salt to taste.
5. Serve warm or at room temperature

Julie's Note:

    I've been lucky enough to have traveled to Syria and also spend time in Damascus, and I've always had a penchant for the Middle Eastern salads. Now I serve them as a main meal, usually with whole grain pita bread on the side.

Tabbouleh

Ingredients   *Serves 6*

     1 cup bulgur wheat, fine grain
     ½ cup fresh mint, chopped
     1 cup of parsley, chopped
     4 green onions, finely chopped
     2 medium tomatoes, diced
     2 cloves garlic, finely chopped
     Juice of 1 lemon
     ¼ cup extra virgin olive oil, or more if needed

1. Place bulgur in a large bowl and add enough hot water to cover.
2. Soak grain for 30 minutes or until tender.
3. Thoroughly squeeze out any excess liquid.
4. Add mint and parsley, toss into the bulgur.
5. Add scallions and tomatoes.
6. In a small bowl, mix garlic and lemon juice, whisk in the oil.
7. Toss the oil dressing over the bulgur salad.
8. Add salt to taste.

Julie's Note:

Lingering in Middle Eastern climes, Tabbouleh is another salad that can add an exotic flare to a meal. Sometimes I like to add 3 tablespoons of toasted pine nuts, and you can substitute bulgur with a cup of cooked quinoa or brown rice for a change.

Fattoush

Ingredients   *Serves 6*

2 whole pita breads
3 cups tomatoes, diced
1 large cucumber, peeled, seeded, and diced
6 green onions, diced
1 green bell pepper, diced
1 yellow pepper, diced
½ cup fresh parsley, chopped
3 tablespoons fresh mint, chopped, or 2 teaspoons dried
2 cloves of garlic, minced
½ cup extra virgin olive oil
¼ cup fresh lemon juice
3 tablespoons pomegranate molasses
Salt and freshly ground black pepper to taste

1. Preheat oven 350 F.
2. Tear the pita into 1-inch pieces, and place on tray in a single layer. Bake for 5-10 minutes, until dry and crisp. Set aside.
3. In a large serving bowl, combine tomatoes, cucumber, scallions, bell peppers, parsley and mint.
4. Whisk together the garlic, olive oil, lemon juice, and pomegranate molasses.
5. Pour over salad. Salt and pepper to taste. Toss. When ready to serve, add pita bread and toss. Serve immediately.

Julie's Note:

From Syria-Lebanon, this salad keeps us in the Middle East for a little longer. The pita bread adds an unusual element, and while other recipes call for the pieces to be fried crisp, I prefer baking them in the oven for a healthier result.

As the salad sits, the pita soaks up the dressing which traditionalists adore. Personally, I like Fattoush while the bread is still crisp.

As a final thought, that pomegranate molasses just makes your taste buds soar. That said, it's still great without!

Edamame Salad

Ingredients   Serves 4

    1 (16 ounce) bag frozen shelled edamame
    ¼ cup raw-unfiltered apple cider vinegar
    2 tablespoons extra virgin olive oil
    1 bunch radishes, thinly sliced
    ½ cup cilantro or parsley, finely chopped
    Salt to taste

1   Heat edamame in saucepan with ½ cup of water until beans are warm.
2   Transfer to serving bowl and toss with vinegar, olive oil, radishes, and cilantro / parsley.
3   Salt to taste.
4   Serve at room temperature or chilled.

Julie's Note:

    Otherwise known as the Japanese version of a peanut, Edamame are soybeans, green, tender and delicious. In this, their purest form, soybeans are a natural source of lecithin which is food for the brain.

Roasted Vegetable Salad

Ingredients   *Serves* 8

Summer Roast:
    3 large zucchini, cut into 1 inch cubes
    3 yellow summer squash, cut into 1 inch cubes
    2 large yellow onions, diced
    2 carrots, chopped
    1 cup finely chopped assorted fresh herbs, such as chives, tarragon, dill,
    cilantro and parsley
    2 cups feta, crumbled (optional)

Fall Roast:
    1 butternut or any winter squash, peeled, seeded, cut into 1 inch cubes
    3 parsnips, chopped
    2 turnips, chopped
    2 large onions, diced
    1 cup finely chopped assorted fresh herbs, such as chives, tarragon, dill,
    cilantro and parsley
    2 cups feta, crumbled (optional)

Olive Oil - Flax Dressing
    ¼ cup extra virgin olive oil
    1/8 cup flax oil (Udo's)
    2 tablespoons fresh lemon juice
    1 tablespoon garlic, chopped

1. Preheat oven 350 degrees F.
2. Place vegetables in a large mixing bowl and toss with olive oil, salt and pepper, to evenly coat.
3. Spread vegetables in one layer in a roasting pan and roast in the oven for 45 minutes or until easily pierces with a knife.
4. Remove from oven and allow to cool for 15 minutes.
5. Place vegetables in a large salad bowl and toss with herbs, olive oil, lemon juice, and garlic.
6. Season to taste with salt and pepper.
7. Toss with cheese and serve.

Julie's Note:

Whatever season you're in, you can get creative and improvise your own version of this salad using what's available. Roasting the vegetables both ignites their flavors and also has a wonderfully grounding effect.

Sea Vegetable Salad

Ingredients   *Serves 4-6*

2 cups dried hijiki
3 tablespoons sesame oil or olive oil
1 medium onion, sliced into thin half-moons
3 carrots, grated
2 tablespoons tamari or shoy1u
3 tablespoons parsley, minced
1/4 cup sunflower seeds, *see page 82 for dry toasting*

1. Rinse hijiki well and set aside.
2. Bring 3 cups water to a boil in a medium saucepan. Remove from heat, add hijiki, cover and let stand for 30 minutes.
3. In a large skillet, saute onions in oil until onions are translucent.
4. Drain hijiki, keeping the water. Add hijiki and tamari to the skillet with onions and saute briefly.
5. Place grated carrots on top of hijiki mixture. Add 1/4 cup of soaking water from the hijiki to the mixture and simmer for 10 minutes, covered.
6. If any liquid remains, cook uncovered over medium heat for a few minutes until nearly dry.
7. Sprinkle parsley over, cover, and steam for 1 minute.
8. To serve, garnish with toasted sunflower seeds, hot, cold, or at room temperature.

Julie's Note:

When you are feeling adventurous, try hijiki! It'll make your hair shiny and your skin radiant, and just looking at it will make you laugh! In Japanese, hijiki means "bearer of wealth and beauty"

Ounce for ounce, sea vegetables are higher in vitamins and minerals than any other class of food. Hijiki is the richest of all the seaweeds in calcium and iron, a good choice when you feel stressed. You may wonder about pollutants in these vegetables. As with other ocean vegetation, sea vegetables will not flourish in polluted areas.

Napa-Asian Chicken Salad

Ingredients   *Serves* 4

    ¼ cup raw-unfiltered apple cider vinegar
    2 tablespoons creamy peanut butter
    1 tablespoon fresh ginger, minced
    2 teaspoon chipotle pepper, puree
    1 tablespoon tamari
    1 tablespoon honey or agave nectar, (optional)
    2 teaspoon toasted sesame oil
    ½ cup extra virgin olive oil
    ½ head Napa cabbage, shredded
    1 head romaine lettuce, shredded
    2 carrots, grated
    ¼ cup fresh cilantro leaves, chopped
    ¼ cup green onions, finely sliced
    2 cups rotisserie chicken, shredded
    ½ cup peanuts, roasted or raw, chopped
    ¼ cup fresh mint leaves, chopped or 2 tablespoons peppermint dried
    1 lime, quartered

1. In a medium bowl, whisk together, vinegar, peanut butter, ginger, chipotle, tamari, honey, sesame oil, and olive oil.
2. Salt and pepper to taste.
3. Combine cabbage, lettuce, carrots, cilantro, and green onions in a large bowl. Add dressing and toss.
4. Transfer to a serving platter, top with chicken, peanuts, and mint.
5. Garnish around platter with lime wedges.

Julie's Note:

    Spicy, colorful and super tasty, this can be a meal in itself. There's also the vegetarian option, replacing the chicken with spicy baked tofu which you'll find at the market in the perishable section.

Curry Chicken Salad

1 large roasted chicken, shredded after removing from bone and skin removed
½ cup celery, chopped
½ small onion, finely chopped
1 tablespoon prepared mango chutney
1 cup mayonnaise
2 tablespoons fresh lemon juice or lime juice
1½ tablespoons curry powder
Salt to taste
½ bunch cilantro or parsley, chopped (optional)
2 ounces silvered almonds, raw or dry roasted

1. Gently combine the chicken, celery, onion, and chutney, in a large bowl.
2. Combine mayo, lemon juice, and curry powder. Add to the chicken mixture and stir.
3. Add salt to taste. Add cilantro / parsley if desired.
4. Serve chilled or at room temperature.
5. Before serving, add almonds.

Tostada Salad

1½ cups cooked pinto beans, black beans or kidney beans
1 head of romaine lettuce, shredded into bite-size pieces
1 tomato, diced
1 avocado, diced
½ cup sliced black olives
¼ cup red onion
Tortillas chips

Chipotle Sour Cream:
1 cup sour cream
1 tablespoon extra virgin olive oil
2 teaspoons finely chopped can chipotles in adobo sauce, (found in the ethnic section in the market)
½ teaspoon salt
1 tablespoon water

In a small bowl mix together ingredients and set aside in the refrigerator ready to serve.

Cilantro Dressing:
1 cup chopped fresh cilantro
½ cup fresh lime juice
½ cup extra virgin olive oil
1 garlic clove, minced
Salt to taste

Blend all ingredients and refrigerate.

Tortilla Chips:
4 large sprouted wheat tortillas, or tortillas of your choice
4 tablespoons of olive oil (optional)

1. Lay out tortillas on baking tray. If using oil: with a pastry brush or napkin, wipe over each tortilla so the surface is covered with oil. Bake at 350 degrees until golden or just almost crisp, around 10 minutes.
2. Cool and then break into pieces. You can precut the tortillas before you bake them if you want a cleaner-edge chip.

To make salad: On a large platter, arrange lettuce, beans, tomatoes, avocado, olives, and onions.

On the side, serve tortilla chips, cilantro dressing and chipotle sour cream.

Optional: Add shredded chicken or grated cow, goat, or soy cheese for topping.

Julie's Note:

Piled high with live, colorful ingredients, Tex-Mex salads can be wonderfully simple and oh so very good to eat.

Simple Salad that Goes with Any Dish

Ingredients   *Serves* 4

      3 cups mixed lettuce greens, torn in bite-size pieces
      1 cup fresh herbs chopped parsley, dill and / or cilantro
      ¼ cup scallions, chopped
      1 cucumber, peeled, seeded and sliced thin
      1 cup sprouts (optional)
      ½ cup of pomegranate seeds (optional)

Mix greens in a large salad bowl and toss with any of the dressings listed.
* Serve with any of dressing of choice. See dressing recipes on page 133.

Julie's Note:

    Sprouts are one of those foods that come in all shapes and sizes -
radish, sunflower, clover, alfalfa, etc. - and are jam packed with nutrition.
For as many varieties there are as many flavors, spicy, mild, hot, earthy, and
it's fun to dive into the world of sprouts and experiment for yourself.
They're a great addition to any salad.

Tuna Salad

 1 can (6 ounces) of water-packed tuna, drained
 ¼ cup parsley, finely chopped
 1 teaspoon capers or 1 teaspoon dill pickle relish
 1 teaspoon green onions or white or purple onions, finely chopped
 2 tablespoons fresh lemon or lime juice
 3 tablespoons extra virgin olive oil, more or less if desired
 Salt to taste

1. In a mixing bowl, place tuna, parsley, capers and onions and mix until blended.
2. Whisk juice and oil and pour over salad and blend. Add salt to taste.
3. Have freshly ground black pepper available when serving.

Variation: Substitute lemon juice and olive oil for 1 heaping tablespoon of mayonaise, more or less as desired.

Julie's Note:

Usually I only serve vegetarian dishes on retreats, but over time I've added some a few with chicken, turkey, eggs and tuna. When this tuna salad is on the menu it's a sure winner for a deluge of rave reviews.

While tuna is a good source of EPA/DHA Omega-3s, it's always a good idea to check to latest mercury contents (look online), especially if you're giving this to kids or are nursing a baby, just to make sure you're within the safety zone. Also, it's fun to substitute salmon for a change, which is right up there at the top in Omega-3s. Good for the brain.

Honey Fruit Salad

Ingredients   *Serves 4-5*

 4 cups combination of sliced strawberries, peaches, apricots, apples,
     and pitted cherries
 2 tablespoons mint, chopped
 ¼ cup toasted pecans, chopped
 3 tablespoons fresh orange juice
 3 tablespoons fresh lemon juice
 2 tablespoons honey
 Mint leaves

1. Combine fruit, mint, and pecans in a serving bowl. Set aside.
2. Whisk together orange juice, lemon juice, and honey.
3. Pour over fruit and toss well.
4. Garnish with mint leaves.
5. Serve at room temperature or chilled.

Julie's Note:

There's fruit salad, and then there's fruit salad. This is fruit salad.
And it's especially good with yogart, kefir or even ice cream. Yum!

Festive Cranberry Salad

    4 cups fresh cranberries, ground in blender
    1 large orange, unpeeled, seeded, ground in blender
    1 cup raw organic sugar, succanat or 2/3 cup honey
    2 (3-ounce) pkg. cranberry or cherry jello
    1 cup boiling water
    1 (15-ounce) can crushed pineapple, un-drained
    1 cup pecans, chopped
    ½ cup celery, diced

1. Combine cranberries, orange and sugar. Cover and chill for 1 hour or chill overnight.
2. In a bowl, dissolve jello, by adding the boiling water, gently stir in cranberry mixture.
3. Add pineapple, pecans, and celery.
4. Spoon mixture into 5-cup jello mold or a serving bowl.
5. Chill until firm.
6. Un-mold on a bed of lettuce or serve from bowl.

Julie's Note:

    This is my all time favorite holiday salad. My Mother makes it every year, and holidays wouldn't be holidays without it.

    Balancing out the tartness of the berries, this is one time when sugar is a must. There are a couple of options of how to get that sweetness. Honey, raw sugar or Succanat which is a trade name for organically grown, dehydrated sugarcane juice.

    Also, if you pick up the jello that's made with agar from the health food store it's a better, healthier option.

Dressings

The following dressings elicit praise and requests for the recipe whenever I serve them. The dressings are best made in advance and allowed to sit for a couple of hours.

Spicy Blue Cheese Dressing

Ingredients   *Makes about 1 ½ cups*

6 ounces blue cheese, crumbled (about 1 ½ cups)
¾ cup mayonnaise
½ cup sour cream or plain yogurt
3 tablespoons fresh lemon juice
1 clove garlic, minced
1 teaspoon honey or agave nectar
1 ½ teaspoon red pepper flakes

Mix all ingredients well and refrigerate for 2 hours before serving.

Lemon Garlic Flax Dressing

Ingredients   *Makes 1 cup*

3 cloves garlic, minced
3 tablespoons Braggs Liquid Aminos
¼ cup fresh lemon juice
½ cup extra virgin olive oil
¼ cup flax oil
Pinch of salt

Combine all ingredients and whisk. Let set for 30 minutes before serving. Whisk again before serving.

Honey Mustard Lime Dressing

Ingredients   *Makes 1 ½ cups*

½ cup extra virgin olive oil
½ cup Dijon mustard
¼ cup honey
3 tablespoons fresh lime juice
2 pinches cayenne pepper

Place all ingredients in a bowl and whisk until creamy.

Avocado Wasabi Dressing

Ingredients   *Makes 1 ½ cups*

2 ripe Hass avocados, peeled and diced
2 tablespoons fresh lemon juice
2 tablespoons wasabi powder
1 teaspoon Braggs Liquid Aminos or tamari
¼ teaspoon salt
½ cup cilantro, finely chopped
½ cup water

Puree all ingredients, except for cilantro, in a blender. May need to use a ½ cup water to make the consistency smooth and creamy. Transfer to a bowl and mix in cilantro.

Lemon Tahini Dressing

Ingredients   *Makes 1 ¼ cups*

> ½ cup tahini
> ¼ cup water
> ¼ cup extra virgin olive oil
> 3 tablespoons fresh lemon juice
> 1 tablespoon raw-unfiltered apple cider vinegar
> 2 garlic cloves, minced
> ½ teaspoon salt
> 1 teaspoon cumin, (optional)

In bowl, whisk together all ingredients until smooth. Let set for 30 minutes.

Sesame Dressing

Ingredients   *Makes 1 cup*

> ½ cup extra virgin olive oil
> ¼ cup toasted sesame seeds
> 2 tablespoons lemon juice
> ½ teaspoon salt
> 1 cup parsley, chopped

Put all ingredients in a blender and blend until nearly smooth.

Raspberry Vinaigrette Dressing

Ingredients   *Makes 1/3 cup*

3 tablespoons extra-virgin olive oil
2 tablespoons raspberry vinegar
11/2 teaspoons Dijon mustard
1 tablespoon chopped shallots
Dash of salt and freshly ground black pepper

Place ingredients in a bowl, whisk together until well blended.

Balsamic Vinaigrette Dressing

Ingredients   *Makes about ¾ cups*

4 teaspoons balsamic vinegar
1 clove garlic, minced
2 teaspoons Dijon mustard
1 teaspoon freshly chopped or dried tarragon
½ cup extra-virgin olive oil
Salt to taste

Combine all ingredients and whisk. May need to whisk again before serving.

Tangy Yogurt Dressing

Ingredients   *Makes ½ cup*

    2 tablespoon lemon juice
    ¼ cup yogurt
    4 tablespoons extra virgin olive oil
    Pinch of salt
    Pinch ground cardamom

Whisk ingredients together until creamy, refrigerate or serve.

Orange Poppy Seed Dressing

Ingredients   *Makes 1 cup*

    1 tablespoon poppy seeds
    ¼ cup frozen orange juice
    ¼ teaspoon white pepper
    2 tablespoons raw unfiltered apple cider vinegar
    ¼ cup extra virgin olive oil
    Salt to taste

Whisk together all ingredients and serve.

Cilantro Dressing

Ingredients   *Makes 1 ¼ cups*

    1 cup fresh cilantro, chopped
    ½ cup lime juice
    ½ cup extra virgin olive oil
    1 clove garlic, minced
    Salt to taste

Blend all ingredients, serve, or refrigerate.

Fiesta Dressing

Ingredients   *Serves 6*

    ½ cup raw-unfiltered apple cider vinegar
    1 tablespoon tamari or Braggs Liquid Aminos
    1 tablespoon honey or agave nectar or raw sugar
    ½ fresh green chile, seeded and minced
    ¼ teaspoon freshly ground black pepper
    2 teaspoons fresh ginger, minced
    Salt to taste

Combine all ingredients, stir and ready to serve.

Tomato, Oil and Vinegar Dressing

Ingredients   *Serves 4*

4 tablespoons tomato juice
3 tablespoons raw-unfiltered apple cider vinegar
4 tablespoons extra-virgin olive oil
Salt and freshly ground black pepper to taste

Mix all ingredients and serve.

Olive oil and Pomegranate Dressing

Ingredients   *Serves 6*

½ cup extra virgin olive oil
¼ cup lemon juice
3 tablespoons pomegranate molasses
2 cloves garlic, minced
2 tablespoons dried peppermint or 3 tablespoons fresh mint, minced
Salt to taste

Mix all ingredients and serve.

Tahini Mint Dressing

Ingredients   *Makes ¾ cup*

    1 tablespoon Braggs Liquid Aminos or tamari
    2 tablespoons tahini
    2 tablespoons extra virgin olive oil
    3 tablespoons lemon juice
    ¼ cup water or more for desired consistency
    1 clove garlic, minced
    ¼ cup fresh mint leaves, minced or 2 heaping tablespoons of dried pepper-
    mint

Puree dressing ingredients until smooth or desired consistency. Serve.

Mustard Citrus Dressing

Ingredients   *Serves 4*

    3 tablespoons extra virgin olive oil
    3 tablespoons lemon juice
    2 teaspoons grated orange zest
    1 teaspoon seeded mustard
    1 tablespoon honey or agave nectar

Whisk all ingredients and serve.

Olive Thyme Dressing

½ cup extra virgin olive oil
1 large shallot, finely chopped
Juice of 1 lemon
Leaves from 10 sprigs of thyme or 1 tablespoon dried
Salt and freshly ground black pepper to taste

Whisk together all ingredients and serve.

Index

L

leeks   17, 20, 48
lemon   24, 26, 34, 37, 38, 39, 42, 46, 49, 52, 57, 60, 61, 70, 71, 74, 75, 76, 80, 82, 83, 8
    6, 87, 88, 89, 92, 94, 98, 99, 100, 101, 102, 104, 105, 113, 115, 116, 117, 118, 120,
    125, 129, 130, 133, 134, 135, 137, 139, 140, 141
lentils
    brown   49
    red   37, 38
lettuce   70, 71, 72, 73, 74, 78, 102, 113, 115, 124, 126, 127, 128, 131
lima beans   34, 36, 44

M

milk   16, 25, 47
Minestrone   30
mint   26, 49, 82, 83, 89, 101, 114, 115, 116, 117, 118, 124, 130, 139, 140
mushrooms
    button   32, 81
    portobello   90
    shitake   40

N

noodles
    bow ties   85
    egg   59
    macaroni   30
    shell   130
    soba   86
    spaghetti   28
    tortellini   32
nuts
    dry roasted   84, 88, 92, 125
    pistachios   82, 98, 114

O

okra   52
orange   73, 82, 98, 130, 131, 137, 140

P

parsley   16, 17, 24, 28, 31, 38, 41, 42, 46, 51, 59, 60, 63, 66, 67, 72, 73,
    79, 80, 83, 89, 92, 94, 107, 109, 112, 113, 115, 116, 117, 118, 120, 128, 129, 135
parsnips   41, 50, 120

About the Author

Julie Marie Brinkley grew up on a farm in western Kentucky. She learned cooking from generations of women cooking with Southern graces. She left Kentucky to travel and work. For over twenty years, she has been attending and cooking for workshops at the Sufi Foundation Retreat Center in New Mexico cooking for groups of seventy to 100 people.

Over the past eight years, she has been head chef for David Elliott's (author of *The Reluctant Healer*) retreats.

Julie and her husband, Greg, have a day spa (East Mountain Health and Healing Retreat) in New Mexico where she enjoys serving her delicious soups and salads, many of which are found in this book. Visit their website at www.LoveJoyHealth.com.

In addition to her cooking skills, Julie is also Registered Nurse since 1983 and Nurse Specialist presently practicing at University of New Mexico Hospital. She is a Sufi Dance Teacher, Certified Yoga Instructor, and mother of two lovely children, Ian Amadeo and Elliott Marie. She shares her talent as a magnicent cook at special events, retreat days and weekend seminars.

Photo by KyleZimmermanPhotography.com

To order more copies of
Comforting Soups Colorful Salads,
go to www.LoveJoyHealth.com

Printed in the United States
68247LVS00004B/11-170

9 780971 068469